HARD TO LOVE

*A guide to loving yourself,
loving God, and loving others.*

NIKKI APPLETON

WESTBOW
PRESS
A DIVISION OF THOMAS NELSON
& ZONDERVAN

Copyright © 2025 Nikki Appleton.

All rights reserved. No part of this book may be used or reproduced by any means, graphic, electronic, or mechanical, including photocopying, recording, taping or by any information storage retrieval system without the written permission of the author except in the case of brief quotations embodied in critical articles and reviews.

WestBow Press books may be ordered through booksellers or by contacting:

WestBow Press
A Division of Thomas Nelson & Zondervan
1663 Liberty Drive
Bloomington, IN 47403
www.westbowpress.com
844-714-3454

Because of the dynamic nature of the Internet, any web addresses or links contained in this book may have changed since publication and may no longer be valid. The views expressed in this work are solely those of the author and do not necessarily reflect the views of the publisher, and the publisher hereby disclaims any responsibility for them.

Any people depicted in stock imagery provided by Getty Images are models, and such images are being used for illustrative purposes only. Certain stock imagery © Getty Images.

ISBN: 979-8-3850-4008-7 (sc)
ISBN: 979-8-3850-4009-4 (e)

Library of Congress Control Number: 2024926506

Print information available on the last page.

WestBow Press rev. date: 1/27/2025

Scripture quotations marked (NIV) are taken from the Holy Bible, NEW INTERNATIONAL VERSION®, NIV® Copyright © 1973, 1978, 1984, 2011 by Biblica, Inc.® Used by permission. All rights reserved worldwide.

Scripture quotations marked (KJV) are taken from the King James Version, public domain.

Scripture quotations marked (AMP) are taken from the Amplified Bible, Copyright © 1954, 1958, 1962, 1964, 1965, 1987 by The Lockman Foundation. Used by permission.

Scripture quotations marked (MSG) are taken from THE MESSAGE, copyright © 1993, 2002, 2018 by Eugene H. Peterson. Used by permission of NavPress. All rights reserved. Represented by Tyndale House Publishers, Inc.

Scripture quotations marked (ESV) are from the ESV® Bible (The Holy Bible, English Standard Version®), copyright © 2001 by Crossway, a publishing ministry of Good News Publishers. Used by permission. All rights reserved.

Scripture quotations marked (NLT) are taken from the Holy Bible, New Living Translation, copyright © 1996, 2004, 2015 by Tyndale House Foundation. Used by permission of Tyndale House Publishers Inc., Carol Stream, Illinois 60188. All rights reserved.

Scripture quotations marked (CEV) are from the Contemporary English Version Copyright © 1991, 1992, 1995 by American Bible Society, Used by Permission.

Scripture quotation marked (GNT) are from the Good News Translation in Today's English Version- Second Edition Copyright © 1992 by American Bible Society. Used by Permission.

Contents

Introduction ix

Part 1 Love Yourself

Chapter 1   Pride 1
Chapter 2   Self-Love 8
Chapter 3   Knowing God 21
Chapter 4   Satan's Not-So-Secret Weapon 33
Chapter 5   Embrace All of You 44

Part 2 Love God

Chapter 6   With All Your Heart 57
Chapter 7   With All Your Soul 67
Chapter 8   With All Your Mind 76
Chapter 9   With All Your Strength 84

Part 3 Love Others

Chapter 10 Who and Why? 97
Chapter 11 Family Ties 107
Chapter 12 The Samaritans 117
Chapter 13 Habits 127

Part 4 Love Your Enemies

Chapter 14 Eye for an Eye 137
Chapter 15 Revenge 148
Chapter 16 Hate Is Easy 158
Chapter 17 Forgiveness, the Real MVP 167
Chapter 18 Final Thoughts 176

Introduction

Love! Love! Love! We hear about it all the time; it's all around us. But is it really? What *is* love? Who do we love? How do we love? Love. Love. Love. If you're anything like me, you may think you have the answers to these questions. But the more I learn and the more I love, the more I realize that we'll never have love truly figured out. One thing I do know for sure is that love isn't easy.

Let's start by bursting a few bubbles, shall we? Love isn't birds singing and lights dimming all around you. Love isn't a feeling you get when someone special comes around. What is love? If you're a millennial, it's possible that you can't ask that question without "What Is Love" by Haddaway playing in your head to visions of side head bobs from *A Night at the Roxbury*. Yes, I get sidetracked easily. Please forgive me and stick around anyway. That question—what is love?—is very complex for a lot of people. Love is not just the thought of one day finding "the one" because love is not limited solely to a romantic concept. It's so much more than that. To me, love is a lot. Love is a verb. Love is action. Love is empathy. Love is something we choose. Love is our calling. Love is God. God is love. But just because I know my what does not mean that the how or the who is easy. Love is hard, and trust me: it's hard to love!

Have you ever had someone in your life who is hard to love? Maybe it's someone at work you don't get along with. Maybe it's someone in your small group who always tries to make everything about them. Maybe it's an in-law who is constantly inserting themselves into your marriage or how you're raising your kids. Maybe it's an abuser who continues to haunt you. Maybe it's a sibling who refuses to take your advice. Maybe it's the barista at your local coffee shop who gives you attitude every morning. Maybe it's yourself. Maybe it's God. Whoever it is for you, we all encounter people who are hard to love because—*spoiler alert*—not one of us is perfect. (Otherwise you wouldn't have picked up this book!)

Love. It's one word. It sounds simple, and oh, how I wish it were. I have found in my walk with Jesus that love is one of the hardest things we are called to do. Love God and love others. It should be easy, right? Be kind to everyone and treat others as you would want to be treated. We all know the Golden Rule. Again, it is all so simple in theory, but when we start to put these concepts and commands into practice, they can be excruciatingly difficult. They also take both time and energy. Trust me. I know. I'm going to assume that you are willing to put in the work or you probably would have stopped reading at the last sentence. Good. I'm glad you're still here.

> The whole point of what we're urging is simply love—love uncontaminated by self-interest and counterfeit faith, a life open to God. (1 Timothy 1:5 MSG)

First Timothy 1:5 says we are to love without self-interest. Pause and really think about that. We are to love others without expecting anything, including reciprocal love, in return. If we are expecting something back, that love is contaminated. Wow. That's eye-opening.

We, as Christians, should be known for how we love. However, more often than not, we are known for what we don't love (who and what we are against) instead of how and who we do love. It's a heartbreaking reality.

Jesus talked a lot about love. In fact, according to the scriptures, it seems that He would rather see His followers have love for one another than any other character trait. In other words, we need to pay attention to this! Love isn't just something we need to read about; it needs to be our focus and our mission.

We are flawed and we are emotional; we're human. Don't

misunderstand this. Having emotions isn't a bad thing. God gave us emotions and I believe they absolutely have purpose, but it's those emotions that make loving so hard. The concept of loving others seems easy to grasp, but how do we put it into action? I ask because without action, it stays just a concept. What practical steps can we take to get closer to loving our neighbors? To loving our enemies? To loving ourselves? To loving God who is, in fact, *love?*

I certainly don't pretend to know everything about love and I'm still learning about all of this love stuff myself. But if you're willing to join me on this journey to discover more about love and about loving yourself, God, and others, I think we'll all be better for it.

After all, the greatest commandment of all is to love God and the second most important commandment is to love your neighbor (others) as yourself. I hope you are ready to dive in because chapter 1 doesn't beat around the bush; we get straight into it.

It's important to note that this book is intended to help you grow so at the end of each chapter are reflection/discussion questions for you to go through. You can work through the book on your own or as part of a small group/Bible study. Either way, I'm looking forward to going on this journey with you.

Part 1
LOVE YOURSELF

Chapter 1
PRIDE

You may be wondering why a book about love is beginning with a chapter on pride. Well, you're not alone. When I first started writing this book, the word *pride* was nowhere in my plans, my thoughts, or my pages.

But God.

Those really are the two best words in the world. We see them throughout scripture, and they always flip the script. I had an idea of what I wanted to write about and share, but God led me in a different direction. It's amazing how we can have our plans ready to go with good intentions leading the charge, but God's plans are higher (and so much better) than ours. We just need to trust Him.

Look at this scripture, for example:

> You rejected this holy, righteous one and instead demanded the release of a murderer. You killed the author of life, **but God** raised him from the dead. And we are witnesses of this fact! (Acts 3:14–15 NLT, emphasis mine)

Talk about a "but God"!

The truth of the matter is I had a plan for this book, but God convicted my heart to acknowledge and address the pridefulness in my own heart. Let me explain that a bit more. I wasn't prideful because I was writing a book. In fact, I was terrified and afraid to fail. This is probably the most vulnerable thing I've ever done. And truth be told, I have never thought of myself as someone who was prideful. But the reason God convicted my heart is because some of the challenges I've had in loving people the way He has called me to have been rooted in pride. I didn't always recognize it at the time, but looking back now, I can see without a doubt that pride poisoned many relationships and situations in my life over the years. Whether it's been wanting to be right, wanting to have the last word, not wanting to be rejected, or not wanting to just let things go and move on. (Bruised ego, anyone?) Those are things that are rooted in pridefulness and we cannot love the way God has called us to love unless we first lay down our pride. I would be doing you (and God!) a disservice if I didn't address this from the jump so don't give up on me yet. Keep reading, and we will set a solid foundation for the chapters to come.

C. S. Lewis said in his book *Mere Christianity*, "For pride is spiritual cancer: it eats up the very possibility of love, or contentment, or even common sense."

Let's start out with the obvious but hard truth: if it weren't for pride, the devil wouldn't be the devil. Think about that. It's because of pride that we have a spiritual enemy in this world. It is because of pride that we are at war with a darkness that we cannot see. And you better believe that he will try to use pride as a weapon in your life because he knows the consequences of pride. His consequences were of the utmost severity—complete separation from God. So if you think that I'm overdoing it by addressing pride before diving into love, think again.

Being prideful is the opposite of what we, as Christians, should be. Think about it. Christianity is about relying on God, recognizing *His* glory and *His* strength, running into *His* arms, and trusting *Him* to carry us through. It's about surrendering ourselves to God and *His* will for our lives. If we have pride in our hearts, we rely on ourselves and our circumstances instead of God.

I need to know more about pride. You need to know more about pride. We all need to know more about pride. Why? Because it's hard to see something when you don't know what you're looking for. Thankfully, the Bible has a lot to say about pride.

> When pride comes, then comes disgrace, but with the humble is wisdom. (Proverbs 11:2 ESV)

Pride leads to disgrace.

> What comes out of a person is what defiles him. For from within, out of the heart of man, come evil thoughts, sexual immorality, theft, murder, adultery, coveting, wickedness, deceit, sensuality, envy, slander, pride, foolishness. All these evil things come from within, and they defile a person. (Mark 7:20–23 ESV)

Pride defiles a person.

> For all that is in the world—the desires of the flesh and the desires of the eyes and pride of life—is not from the Father but is from the world. (1 John 2:16 ESV)

Pride is not from God.

> But he gives us more grace. That is why Scripture says, "God opposes the proud but gives grace to the humble." (James 4:6 NLT)

God opposes pride.

> The fear of the LORD is hatred of evil.
> Pride and arrogance and the way of evil
> and perverted speech I hate. (Proverbs 8:13 ESV)

Pride is evil.

Do I need to keep going? The Bible is pretty clear on this subject.

Now I think it's important to make a distinction here. Pridefulness is different from feeling a sense of accomplishment for reaching a goal or overcoming something challenging. Pridefulness, in the sense that we are talking about, is pride paired with the absence of humility. It's cockiness that is in a long-term relationship with entitlement. Having confidence (and teaching our kids to have confidence, which I think is incredibly important) is also different from pride. The apostle Paul talks about his confidence when he states in Philippians 4:13 (NKJV), "I can do all things through Christ who strengthens me." Paul is confident in himself because he knows his source. He knows that he can do anything with God and nothing without Him. But he didn't come by this confidence or humility easily. Paul was honest about his struggle with pride as well. In 2 Corinthians he says,

> If I wanted to boast, I would be no fool in doing so, because I would be telling the truth. But I won't do it, because I don't want anyone to give me credit beyond what they can see in my life or hear in my message, even though I have received such wonderful revelations from God. So to keep me from becoming proud, I was given a thorn in my flesh, a messenger from Satan to torment me and keep me from becoming proud.
>
> Three different times I begged the Lord to take it away. Each time he said, "My grace is all you need. My power works best in weakness." So now I am glad to boast about my weaknesses, so that the power of Christ can work through me. That's why I take pleasure in my weaknesses, and in the insults, hardships, persecutions, and troubles that I suffer for Christ. For when I am weak, then I am strong. (2 Corinthians 12:6–10 NLT)

Hard to Love

If I look at what pride has looked like in my life, in terms of something that has prevented me from loving in the way God has called me to love, it started with my unconscious tendency to be defensive.

Allow me, for a moment, to switch into a parenting mindset. When I had my daughter, my precious firstborn, I got oodles of unsolicited advice, it seemed, from anyone who crossed my path. Some new moms may think, *Great. This all very helpful and I'll take it into consideration and do what's best for our family.* But not me. Nope. I would get defensive because I took it as a personal attack on my ability to be a good mom. It sounds absurd when I write it out now, but that's honestly how I felt at the time. And that was my pride. *I don't need your help; I don't need anyone's help! I can do this. I'm perfectly capable. I know what I'm doing!* Pride and hormones … not my finest moments. The truth is I did need help. Being a new parent is exhausting. Admitting that I needed help was so hard for me though. Why? Because … pride.

I never wanted to admit I needed help because I didn't want to be seen as weak. That's what I equated with help—admitting defeat. It's a mindset that I had from an early age. My parents got divorced when I was only a year old and after that, my mom, being a single mom, tried to prepare me for the world. I remember her constantly telling me that I needed to get an education because I needed to be able to take care of myself. I could be left on my own, a single mom, having to provide for my kids with no help and I needed to prepare for that possibility. Basically I was taught that I couldn't rely on anyone but myself. Not exactly a heavenly or biblical mindset. But I wasn't raised with any religious beliefs. My mom did the absolute best she could, and I am so incredibly thankful for her. She honestly believed she was protecting me and preparing me for life and I don't blame her for that at all. It's a hard world out there.

That said, this sense of independence, self-reliance, and pride was instilled in me at a young age, and because of that, I have to check myself and be very self-aware because the devil loves to use pride against me. In fact, I think it's his favorite tool. But the good news is that there is freedom from pride and we can all do better—be better versions of ourselves—relying and trusting in God, our Father.

Let's circle back to C. S. Lewis. Again, from his book *Mere Christianity*, Lewis says, "A proud man is always looking down on things and people; and, of course, as long as you are looking down, you cannot see something that is above you."

As long as we are prideful, we are focused on ourselves; we cannot focus on God and the things of God. If we are only looking to ourselves and only relying on ourselves, we can't possibly be looking to God. Because of this, before turning the page, we are going to pray.

> Heavenly Father,
> I humbly come before You and lay down my pride.
> I ask You to please show me, by Your Spirit, where there is pridefulness in my life.
> [Pause and see what comes to mind.]
> I repent from this pridefulness [be specific] and ask You to please forgive me.
> Help me to keep a humble heart and glorify Your name above all else.
> In Jesus's name I pray. Amen.

If nothing came to mind in that prayer, don't worry. Keep an open heart, and even come back to this prayer as you go through these pages and be prepared for God to reveal things to you as He sees fit.

Now let's take the apostle Paul's words to heart as we explore love.

> Don't be selfish; don't try to impress others. Be humble, thinking of others as better than yourselves.
> (Philippians 2:3 NLT)

After all, in order to love—in any way, shape, or form—we need to be vulnerable. In order to be vulnerable, we need to lay down our pride.

I love how C. S. Lewis put it in *The Four Loves*.

> To love at all is to be vulnerable. Love anything and your heart will be wrung and possibly broken. If you want to make sure of keeping it intact you must give it to no one, not even an animal. Wrap it carefully round with hobbies and little luxuries; avoid all entanglements. Lock it up safe in the casket or coffin of your selfishness. But in that casket, safe, dark, motionless, airless, it will change. It will not be broken; it will become unbreakable, impenetrable, irredeemable. To love is to be vulnerable.

Now, let's get lovin'!

Reflection/Discussion Questions

- What stood out to you the most in this chapter?
- Have you ever contemplated the connection between pride and love?
- Did the prayer at the end of the chapter bring anything to mind about where you could have pridefulness in your life?
- Do you struggle to learn from others or accept wisdom or advice from others?
- Do you have a hard time asking for help?
- Do you find it difficult to submit to authority?

Chapter 2
SELF-LOVE

So here we are. Flawed humans with instructions to love others the way a perfect God loves us. Huh. Well friend, if you have no idea where to start, you're in good company. This is something that a lot of people—Christians and non-Christians alike—struggle with. I wish I could tell you that I didn't also struggle with this, but I do.

First things first, we need to take off our love goggles. We all have them. We all have our own idea of what love is, based on our own experiences and our own lives. For most of us, we have some experiences with love that are good and some experiences with love that are not. These experiences shape our thoughts and opinions of what love is and what it looks like, as well as how we give and receive love.

Personally, I've had a rather tumultuous relationship with love throughout my life. It took me over twenty years to learn to love myself, and if I'm honest, I'm still learning to. I feel like I always will be. Learning to love ourselves is definitely a journey. One thing I can confirm from experience, and you've probably heard somewhere before, is that you can't love anyone else—I mean truly love them—until you love yourself. For many of us, the journey to self-love is long and difficult with bumpy and dangerous terrain filled with twists and turns. But something else I can tell you from experience is that it's worth it. Without a doubt, 100 percent, it is absolutely worth it.

So let's pause for a moment and look in the mirror. Seriously, get up and look in the mirror, or at least open your phone's front camera. Who do you see looking back at you? Are you happy with that person? Do you love who you see?

Notice I asked if you love *"who"* you see, not *"what"* you see. That is intentional because as people, as spiritual beings, we are so much more than our bodies, our faces, our outside appearance. You don't have to love that zit on your forehead, that receding hairline, or that extra ten pounds that seemed to just show up one day and refuses to leave. You don't need to love those things in order to love yourself. (Thank goodness for that!) You are so much more than your physical characteristics! Now think about this question: what does the term *self-love* mean to you? If you're someone who has already started this journey, I commend you. I truly believe that self-love is an ongoing process so I hope you'll stay with me over the next few chapters, really dig in, and do a self-check on self-love.

What is self-love?

The definition of *self-love,* according to merriam-webster.com, is this: love of self, such as an appreciation of one's own worth or virtue.

Self-love is an appreciation of your worth; I would even dare to say that it's an understanding that *you have worth.* Why is that so important? Let's talk about it. If you don't believe that you have value or worth, how can you see the value and worth in others? How can you accept real love from someone—or even from God—when you don't believe you have value or deserve to be loved? So I'll say it again. You can't truly love others until you love yourself. Also, if you can't see your own worth, you will allow people to treat you as worthless when, in reality, you are a beautiful child of God who is loved and adored by your Heavenly Father.

Read this portion of Psalm 139; it is a beautiful depiction of how loved you are by your Creator.

> For the choir director: A psalm of David.
> O Lord, you have examined my heart
>   and know everything about me.
> You know when I sit down or stand up.

You know my thoughts even when I'm far away.
You see me when I travel
   and when I rest at home.
   You know everything I do.
You know what I am going to say
   even before I say it, Lord.
You go before me and follow me.
   You place your hand of blessing on my head.
Such knowledge is too wonderful for me,
   too great for me to understand!

I can never escape from your Spirit!
   I can never get away from your presence!
If I go up to heaven, you are there;
   if I go down to the grave, you are there.
If I ride the wings of the morning,
   if I dwell by the farthest oceans,
even there your hand will guide me,
   and your strength will support me.
I could ask the darkness to hide me
   and the light around me to become night—
but even in darkness I cannot hide from you.
To you the night shines as bright as day.
   Darkness and light are the same to you.

You made all the delicate, inner parts of my body
   and knit me together in my mother's womb.
Thank you for making me so wonderfully complex!
   Your workmanship is marvelous—how well I
   know it.
You watched me as I was being formed in utter
seclusion,
   as I was woven together in the dark of the womb.

You saw me before I was born.
> Every day of my life was recorded in your book.
Every moment was laid out
> before a single day had passed.

How precious are your thoughts about me, O God.
> They cannot be numbered!
I can't even count them;
> they outnumber the grains of sand!
And when I wake up,
> you are still with me! (Psalm 139:1–18 NLT)

How precious are His thoughts about you! How precious are His thoughts about me! His precious thoughts about us outnumber the grains of sand! Incredible.

It still breaks my heart to admit it, but I spent a good portion of my life not loving myself. In fact, for a good portion of my years on earth, I loathed myself. That may be an extreme that you are lucky enough to not have encountered, but either way, I didn't like myself—never mind love myself. But why was it so hard for me to love myself anyway? Why was that such a struggle (because honestly, it was a very long and painful struggle)?

If you've ever been around a toddler, you know that they are sponges. They are incredibly observant and pick up anything and everything going on around them—especially the stuff you wish they wouldn't! When my daughter was three, she started mimicking my facial expressions and the sarcastic tones in my voice in certain situations and it was not pleasant. Trust me: it was not an easy mirror to look into! But in doing this, she actually started holding me accountable and helped me see that I needed to change my habits and try to do better. Since children are learning and developing every minute of every day, it stands to reason that a lot of concepts and feelings about ourselves and who we are actually begin to develop when we're just kids.

I can attest to this because when I was about five years old, my mom put me in a ballet class. Fun, right? *Who doesn't love a group of tiny humans in tutus?* Unfortunately, my one and only memory from that ballet class was my teacher poking my stomach and telling me, "Suck in that Santa Claus belly." Yep, that's it. I don't remember the music, the outfits (not a single tutu), the dances—nothing. And that is actually very telling considering that I remember all of those details from my jazz class I also took at that age. We performed to Paula Abdul in black and yellow sparkly outfits and it was amazing. But not ballet. Nothing. All I remember from ballet class is that one single comment. From that day forward, I had a complex. I didn't know it at the time, but I spent the next twentysomething years of my life being overly self-conscious of my stomach and how it looked at all times. What a terrible way to live—especially as a child and a teenager!

First of all, what a terrible thing to say to a child! But I honestly don't think that dance teacher meant any harm and never thought for a moment that I'd be writing about her and how she traumatized me as a very young child in her care. But here we are, and if that's not proof that our words have power, I don't know what is. So please, if you have children in your life, be overly careful with your words. I know sometimes things are said in the heat of the moment or without thinking of the consequences, but those moments open the door for us to humble ourselves, apologize, and teach our children how important words are, how important kindness is, and how important it is to apologize when we've done something wrong. And if we model that for our children, our nieces and nephews, all the kids in our lives, they will have a better chance of learning those same habits in their own lives and that is something that is truly invaluable.

OK, that was a sidebar, but I truly believe we need to do everything in our power to help the next generation learn to love themselves from a young age because it will serve them well for their entire lives!

Hard to Love

Back to how our opinions of ourselves begin to form when we are young …

On a more severe level, I was programmed from a very young age to believe that my only worth was in what boys/men thought of me. This belief came from being molested at a young age by a boy at a day home. I won't get into the details except to say that this trauma programmed my brain from a very young age to believe untrue things about myself. For too many years than I care to admit, my only sense of self-worth came from the attention and affection I received from boys/men. That was it. I can tell you with absolute certainty that when your sense of worth and value depends solely on other people and what they think of you, you will never love yourself and you will always be miserable inside. The reason I say that is because people will always let you down. We are all human and we are all flawed. There's no way around it. You can put on a happy face, you can project a false sense of confidence, you can pretend all you want, but there will always be something missing and you will never fully measure up. I know this beyond a shadow of a doubt because I lived it every single day for many years of my life. I was a body first, a person second. Even writing that sentence brings tears to my eyes because no child, teenager, or adult should ever feel like that, and it breaks my heart knowing that there are still so many people in this world who do.

As you can imagine, that programming in my brain led to all kinds of issues. I was never good enough for anyone. I was never enough, period. I never got enough attention. I was never pretty enough or smart enough or funny enough. I was just never enough. That constant bombardment of failure, of never measuring up, led to depression, alcohol abuse, suicidal thoughts, self-harm, toxic relationship after toxic relationship, and the list goes on. I was searching for validation from the world that I was worth something—anything—but I always came up short. Every time I thought I couldn't hurt anymore, I couldn't break anymore, I did. It was painful; it was lonely; it was a prison; it was my life. I wore a mask everywhere I went. *I'm tough. I don't care what you think. I'm confident. I'm happy with my choices, and I love my life.* Underneath that mask, I was so broken that I never thought I'd be able to smile from a place of sincerity. Behind closed doors I cried, I screamed, and I cut myself, desperately trying to numb the pain I felt inside by inflicting pain on the outside. I never thought I could possibly know what it felt like to feel happy, secure, and loved. Never. I didn't feel like I deserved to.

I hurt and abused my body time and time again. Sometimes, as I mentioned, to distract from the inner turmoil I felt, but I also hurt myself because I believed that's what I deserved. I hurt others too. I couldn't give anyone genuine love because I didn't love myself. I didn't understand love. I believed that physical affection was love and you can imagine the pain and trauma that came from the realization that it wasn't. I also didn't feel worthy of love. I never had. In fact, I felt so unworthy of love that I was certain no one could ever truly love me and that no one would ever want to be loved by me. I tried to be who I thought other people wanted me to be—someone they could actually love. I couldn't be myself because I hated myself and believed that if others got to know the real me, they would too. I wasn't worth loving so I acted in whatever way I thought people wanted me to act. It was exhausting, and as I'm sure you can imagine, it was always disappointing.

All of that to say that we all have our traumas. We all have our programming. Do you know what yours is? Have you taken time to pray about it and ask God to reveal it to you? And once you've done that, how do you move past it in order to break free and reprogram yourself on your own terms? How did someone as broken as me go from loathing my very being and wanting to die—literally wanting to die—to loving myself and appreciating, even celebrating, my imperfections? The journey was (and still is) long, but the answer is simple. The answer, ironically, is love. Specifically, the love of Jesus.

My heart needed some serious rehabilitation. In fact, we all need heart rehab. Why? Because we live in a broken world with broken people. If you injure your knee, you need to go to physiotherapy to rehabilitate that knee. After getting injured, it's limited in what it can do and affects your everyday life so you put in the hard work to get it back to its full potential again. After all, you wouldn't want to live with an injury forever if you didn't have to, right? The same goes for our hearts. While we may have broken, bruised, and scarred hearts, we don't have to stay in and live in that hurt. The Bible says,

> He heals the brokenhearted
> And binds up their wounds [healing their pain and comforting their sorrow]. (Psalm 147:3 AMP)

I don't know about you, but I sure want God to do that for me!

I can tell you from experience, and I hope it will encourage you today, that God never wastes a hurt. I know that when you're in the midst of the hurt and pain, it doesn't feel that way but it's true. You will get through it and other people will find healing because of your testimony. Your greatest life messages and your most effective ministry will come out of your deepest hurts or what you might consider your "mess." But before you can help other people through their hurts, you have to get through yours.

Most, if not all, of our hurts stem from some kind of resentment—someone did something to us, someone hurt us. We hold on to some kind of grudge, offense, anger, or hurt directed at that person. We'll get into forgiveness and loving others (including our enemies) more in later chapters.

The other kind of hurt that we can hold on to is called shame. It's when we do something that we feel bad about or we blame ourselves for. It's when we feel embarrassed or ashamed about our circumstances or lives and hold on so tightly to that shame, that feeling that we are not good enough, not worthy, that it becomes part of our identity. We think we don't deserve forgiveness or love.

I need you to know that shame and condemnation are not from God. Shame is a crafty tactic the devil uses to keep us stuck, and when we live in shame and condemnation, we are essentially telling Jesus that what He did on the cross wasn't quite good enough. It may be good enough for others—His blood can cover the sins of other people, just not mine.

Conviction is different from shame as it is rooted in our faith and our beliefs about God. Conviction is something that God uses to help us change our lives and behaviors to align with His Word and His will. But living in shame and condemnation—being stuck in that cycle and that hopelessness—is not from God and it is not something God wants for you or your life.

The Bible teaches us,

> Before I confessed my sins, my bones felt limp, and I groaned all day long. Night and day your hand weighed heavily on me, and my strength was gone as in the summer heat. So I confessed my sins and told them all to you. I said, "I'll tell the LORD each one of my sins." Then you forgave me and took away my guilt. (Psalm 32:3–5 CEV).

David talks about the physical toll that his sin and his internal turmoil took on this body. Isn't that interesting? Well, an October 2013 study by scientists at Princeton University and the University of Waterloo scientifically verified what David said centuries earlier: feelings of being physically "weighed down" by guilt are real.[1]

I hope you're beginning to see how important it is for us to rehab our hearts.

I challenge you to start by grabbing a pencil and paper and asking God to bring to mind your shame and any sin in your life that you might not even be aware of. Take your time. Don't rush it. Be specific.

Once you've done that, confess those things to God and ask

---

[1] https://journals.plos.org/plosone/article?id=10.1371/journal.pone.0069546.

Hard to Love

for forgiveness. And here's the golden ticket: believe that God will actually forgive you. Believe that His love is bigger than whatever sin or shame you are dealing with. Ask Him to forgive you based on what he promises in the Bible (1 John 1:9). Don't beg. Don't bargain. Just believe that God is able and willing to forgive you. And then know that as God forgives you, you must also forgive—and He can help with this. You aren't on your own.

It's OK to feel hurt. We are human and have feelings. In fact, we can take those emotions to God. He cares about how we feel! In the book of Psalms it says,

> O my people, trust in him at all times.
> Pour out your heart to him,
> for God is our refuge. (Psalm 62:8 NLT)

You might be angry with God for things that have happened in your past. He knows it, you know it, but you won't admit it. The starting point is to say, "God, I'm still upset. I'm angry that this happened!" God's not going to fry you with a thunderbolt if you confess your feelings. He already knows how you feel. You just start the healing process and open the lines of communication with your Creator by coming to terms with it and admitting it to Him.

Once you write down and admit the shame and sin in your life, you can begin to forgive yourself. It's not easy, but it's the only way to truly free yourself from the weight of those burdens. Personally, I found forgiving myself to be one of the hardest things I've ever done. We'll get into forgiving others in a later chapter because that obviously has challenges as well, but when it comes to self-love, we need to find a way to forgive ourselves. And believe me: forgiveness can take a lot of work. But it's worth it and God will be with you to encourage you and strengthen you along the way.

Often when the subject of confession is brought up, people get squirmy and nervous. More often than not, we are afraid that we're going to be judged for what we say. You need to make the choice of whether you want to move past what is holding you back and get right with God or if you want to live in fear of what others may think. I can tell you from personal experience that telling someone (someone I trust) all my dirty laundry was the most freeing experience ever!

> The fear of human opinion disables; trusting in God protects you from that. (Proverbs 29:25 MSG)

We can't suffer in secret. It only gets worse when we do. In another psalm, David explains what happened when he tried to keep his struggles a secret.

> The Confession of a Sufferer
> I said, "I will be careful about what I do
> and will not let my tongue make me sin;
> I will not say anything
> while evil people are near."
> I kept quiet, not saying a word,
> not even about anything good!
> But my suffering only grew worse,
> and I was overcome with anxiety.
> The more I thought, the more troubled I became;
> I could not keep from asking:
> "Lord, how long will I live?
> When will I die?
> Tell me how soon my life will end." (Psalm 39:1–4 GNT)

The good news is that God cares about you. I care about you too. And there is hope. You don't have to stay in that cycle of pain, anxiety, and fear. But first you've got to stop being silent. You've got to speak up and tell someone you trust. You've got to bring it into the light so that God can begin to lead you into healing and use your broken pieces to create a beautiful mosaic masterpiece!

Something else I want to mention as a side note is that I needed to work through the shame tied to the trauma I experienced in my childhood and it was hard. I had to fight the voices in my head that tried telling me that it wasn't that big of a deal. That's just something kids do. I had to fight to believe that my trauma was real, that it was valid, and that the fear and the shame I remember feeling as a child in that situation were not normal. Don't let anyone minimize your trauma or your experiences. They are yours and only you know how they've affected you. Fight for your mental health and your freedom. Fight to reprogram yourself. With God, all things are possible!

Sample Prayer

>Heavenly Father,
>
>Thank You for loving me in the way that only You can. Thank You for loving me and my imperfections. Thank You that You are the definition of love. I ask You, Lord, to please reveal to me where I have been programmed to not love myself. Help me to understand what needs to change and what I need to work on. Search my soul, oh Lord, and help me on this journey of loving myself and coming to know myself as Your beloved child. I repent from my sin [be specific here] and help me let go of the shame and condemnation I've been carrying. I give it all to You, Lord.
>
>In Jesus's name, amen.

Reflection/Discussion Questions

- Do you love yourself beyond your physical characteristics? Do you love who you are?
- Do you believe that your Heavenly Father loves you?
- Do you believe you have worth?
- Did someone tell you something as a child (or even as an adult) that affects how you see yourself today? If so, what did they say and how can you start to move past it?
- Have you ever felt like a body first and a person second?
- Have you experienced any traumas that have programmed you to believe negative things about yourself?
- Do you struggle with feelings of shame or condemnation?

Chapter 3
KNOWING GOD

Real talk? Self-love is hard. I truly believe that loving yourself is a lifelong journey.

As I've mentioned, I used to really struggle with accepting that I was loveable, worthy of love. I couldn't accept God's love because I didn't know *how to* accept it. In reality, I didn't know how to accept real love from people, never mind God. I always assumed that they expected something from me. After all, that's what my life experiences had taught me. And when you've been taught time and time again that you don't deserve love and that you aren't worthy of love, that you're only good for one thing, you can't be expected to all of a sudden embrace something more, something deeper, with the snap of a finger. Why would God love me when no one else could or would? I couldn't think of a single reason why. I had no real self-worth and that made me feel like I didn't deserve love. In my mind, I deserved nothing of the sort.

The worst part is that once I became a Christian in my early twenties, I knew the answer to these questions. How could God love me when no one else could? Because He's God. How could I trust God not to let me down like everyone else in my life? Because He's God. In my head I knew these things, but I had a hard time accepting them in my heart. But that didn't mean I wasn't going to try. I desperately wanted to change my perception of myself and truly accept and embrace God's love for me so I knew that somehow I had to get that head knowledge into my heart.

Maybe you're like me and you know this is something you need to do (or do more of) but don't know where to start. There's absolutely no shame in that; you're definitely not alone. I realized that I needed to better understand and grasp the head knowledge of "Because He's God" and turn it into my reality. What better way to do that than to get to *know* God? This is where His Word is absolutely crucial because it dives into God's character and tells us so much about Him. It explains who He truly is, His character, His heart, all of it.

One of the first things we need to remember is that God created us and He doesn't make mistakes. If you are a Christian, someone who believes in the Holy Trinity—Father, Son, and Spirit—you should know that statement to be true. And He says incredible things about us throughout the Bible! And yet somehow, despite all that knowledge and reinforcement, we question ourselves. We question our worth. Why? Is it simply human nature or is it because we are constantly bombarded with messages that are contrary to the Bible and to what God says about us? Let's be honest. It's a harsh world we live in. But the Bible tells us not to question who we are.

> On the contrary, who are you, O man, who answers [arrogantly] back to God and dares to defy Him? Will the thing which is formed say to him who formed it, "Why have you made me like this?" (Romans 9:20 AMP)

The Bible says not to question God as to why He made us the way we are, and if you think about it, that is an incredibly valid point. Who are we to question the Almighty and Holy One? Who are we to question the Creator, the One who created not only us but also the heavens and the earth? I ask myself this on a regular basis. It took a really long time for me to get this concept from a piece of head knowledge, something I read, to something transformative, tattooed on my heart.

God created us as we are. If you call yourself a Christian, hopefully you are already somewhat familiar with God's character; He does not lie and He does not make mistakes. But don't feel bad if you're not. We are all still learning. Either way, I recommend pulling out your Bible and taking a deep dive into the Word. *He is a perfect God;* there is no denying it. Looking at God's character can help us to not only understand Him but also His intentions and His work (we are His masterpieces!) so much better. So let's look at God's character.

God is holy.

> Each of the four living creatures had six wings and was covered with eyes all around, even under its wings. Day and night they never stop saying: "Holy, holy, holy is the Lord God Almighty," who was, and is, and is to come. (Revelation 4:8 NIV)

God is just.

> He is the Rock, his works are perfect, and all his ways are just. A faithful God who does no wrong, upright and just is he. (Deuteronomy 32:4 NIV)

God is truth.

> Jesus answered, "I am the way and the truth and the life. No one comes to the Father except through me." (John 14:6 NIV)

God is love.

> And so we know and rely on the love God has for us. God is love. Whoever lives in love lives in God, and God in them. (1 John 4:16 NIV)

God is good.

> "Why do you call me good?" Jesus answered. "No one is good—except God alone." (Mark 10:18 NIV)

God is infinite.

> He is before all things, and in him all things hold together. (Colossians 1:17 NIV)

God is omnipotent.

> By the word of the Lord the heavens were made, their starry host by the breath of his mouth. (Psalm 33:6 NIV)

God is omniscient.

> Remember the former things, those of long ago;
>   I am God, and there is no other;
>   I am God, and there is none like me.
> I make known the end from the beginning,
>   from ancient times, what is still to come.
> I say, "My purpose will stand,
>   and I will do all that I please." (Isaiah 46:9–10 NIV)

God is wise.

> Oh, the depth of the riches of the wisdom and knowledge of God! How unsearchable his judgments, and his paths beyond tracing out! (Romans 11:33 NIV)

God is faithful.

> If we are faithless, he remains faithful, for he cannot disown himself. (2 Timothy 2:13 (NIV)

Keep in mind that this is by no means a comprehensive list. He is also merciful, gracious, perfect, glorious, and so much more.

Do we serve an amazing God or what? If I believe God is all of those things, how can I believe that everything He does makes sense and is good ... except me? Could I be the one exception to His perfection? That's actually a thought rooted in pride. He made everyone and everything else right, but I am the one exception because He messed up on me. What? Really? By believing that, we are blatantly contradicting our faith in God. Once you grasp that, it can drastically change your way of thinking. *We can't truly love God and dislike ourselves.* Why? Because God made us. Even when we think we don't measure up, even when we have a laundry list of things we would change about ourselves, *God loves us where we are, as we are.* You are not a surprise to God. He knows every detail about you (even the stuff we would change if we could), and He loves you unconditionally.

> I praise you, for I am fearfully and wonderfully made. Wonderful are your works; my soul knows it very well. (Psalm 139:14 ESV)

> See what kind of love the Father has given to us, that we should be called children of God; and so we are. The reason why the world does not know us is that it did not know him. (1 John 3:1 ESV)

> Before I formed you in the womb I knew you, and before you were born I consecrated you; I appointed you a prophet to the nations. (Jeremiah 1:5 ESV)

The Bible says some pretty cool stuff about us, doesn't it? The next time you catch yourself saying, "I wish I was more ..." or "I wish I wasn't ..." remember what the Bible says about you.

With all of that said and with all of that knowledge in our heads, it can still be challenging to move it from head knowledge to heart knowledge. Heart knowledge is when we know beyond the shadow of a doubt that it is true and real. It moves from something we know to being part of who we are.

Head knowledge can be easily shifted by our emotions and circumstances. Let me give you an example. For me, the existence of God is heart knowledge. I have faith because I know He's real. Even when my life isn't going the way I planned. Even when my cousin, who was like a brother to me, dies suddenly and my world is turned upside down, I don't question the existence or the goodness of God. That's heart knowledge. Head knowledge is very different. I know people who have completely walked away from their faith because someone in the church hurt their feelings, offended them, or they went through a rough patch in their lives. That's thinking God is real or wanting Him to be real but not knowing it deep in your soul. There's a significant difference.

Here's another way of putting it:

> *Head knowledge* is knowing what the Bible says about God.

> *Heart knowledge* is knowing God intimately and having a personal relationship with Him.

There's a big difference.

Now let's look at feelings quickly. Don't get me wrong. Our ability to feel emotions is part of what makes us who we are. God gave us emotions, and because of that, feelings aren't wrong. In fact, they are part of what makes us human. Jesus had emotions. He felt anger, frustration, compassion, sorrow, joy, love, and more. We will all experience emotions; that is unavoidable. It's part of the beauty of being human. What we *can* avoid is letting our emotions jump into the driver's seat of our lives.

The shortest verse in the Bible, and one of favorites for many reasons, is John 11:35 (NIV), which says, "Jesus wept." It's simple;

Hard to Love

it's beautiful; it's human. I don't think there's a verse in the Bible that humanizes Jesus more than this. It shows us that He went through the same things we did. He felt hurt and sad. The word *wept* is so chock-full of emotion. That verse wouldn't have the same impact if it said, "Jesus cried." It's just not the same. Also, the context of this verse is so important. Jesus wept when he heard the news that his friend Lazarus had died. You might be familiar with the rest of this well-known story in the Bible. After He wept, Jesus then went on to raise Lazarus from the dead. He knew that He was going to raise Lazarus from the dead so He knew that He would see his friend again. Despite that, Jesus still took time to weep. He allowed Himself to feel the emotions that came up in the moment and then He did what He was there to do: a miracle. Jesus should always be our example in everything we do, and through Jesus's example, we can see that our feelings are part of what makes us human. We can feel our feelings, but we must also be able to move forward in faith, just like Jesus did.

In chapter 11 I'll mention feelings and emotions again, as well as the importance of overcoming them. For now, I just want to discuss the difference between feelings and truth. We know that *God's Word is truth*. Sometimes our emotions can be grounded in truth, and sometimes they are not. What we need to be hyperaware of is that *feelings are not facts*.

On our journey to loving ourselves, we need to recognize that. The Bible says,

> Trust in the Lord with all your heart;
>   do not depend on your own understanding.
> Seek his will in all you do,
>   and he will show you which path to take. (Proverbs 3:5–6 NLT)

We are to trust in the Lord, not ourselves, our flesh, our feelings. Trust in the Lord. However, I realize that's easier said than done. Emotions can be incredibly strong and powerful at times, even all-consuming, especially when we aren't aware of what is coming from God and what is coming from our flesh.

Living by the Spirit's Power

> So I say, let the Holy Spirit guide your lives. Then you won't be doing what your sinful nature craves. The sinful nature wants to do evil, which is just the opposite of what the Spirit wants. And the Spirit gives us desires that are the opposite of what the sinful nature desires. These two forces are constantly fighting each other, so you are not free to carry out your good intentions. But when you are directed by the Spirit, you are not under obligation to the law of Moses.
>
> When you follow the desires of your sinful nature, the results are very clear: sexual immorality, impurity, lustful pleasures, idolatry, sorcery, hostility, quarreling, jealousy, outbursts of anger, selfish ambition, dissension, division, envy, drunkenness, wild parties, and other sins like these. Let me tell you again, as I have before, that anyone living that sort of life will not inherit the Kingdom of God.
>
> But the Holy Spirit produces this kind of fruit in our lives: love, joy, peace, patience, kindness, goodness, faithfulness, gentleness, and self-control. There is no law against these things!
>
> Those who belong to Christ Jesus have nailed the passions and desires of their sinful nature to his cross and crucified them there. (Galatians 5:16–24 NLT)

Hard to Love

This passage of scripture is so powerful. Yes, I am aware that it doesn't explicitly say that we can't always trust our feelings, but what it does say is that we are to let the Holy Spirit guide our lives. If we don't, our sinful nature can take over, and that includes feelings, such as anger and jealousy. But when we put the Holy Spirit in the driver's seat, that is when we experience love, joy, peace, and other incredible things! Allowing ourselves to be led by the Holy Spirit is critical to our self-love journey because the Holy Spirit helps us to discern what is from God and what is not. When I look in the mirror and get depressed by what I see, is that from God? Of course not! And if I allow the Holy Spirit to speak to me and guide me, He will reassure me of that.

If being led by the Spirit and being in constant relationship with Him is something that is new to you, here are a few steps to get you started. All of these steps are equally important so please don't think you can simply skate by with only doing one and that will change your life. It may help a bit, but true change is a choice and it takes work. Self-love takes work. Getting to know God takes work. But you can't truly have the former without the latter.

Step 1: Pray. Start your day by opening your heart to God and asking Him to guide you today. Pray to be Spirit led and to hear God's voice above all else, including your own thoughts and feelings.

Step 2: Read your Bible. Sounds simple, right? You'd be surprised at how many Christians don't read their Bible daily. But we can't get closer to God without knowing more about Him, and the way we do that is through scripture. If you find this difficult or you're having a hard time fitting it into your schedule, consider listening to an audio Bible. I still think it's vital to have a hard copy Bible in your home that you open and can mark up, highlight, study, write notes in, etc. But if you're in a season where you're finding it challenging to make time for that (shout out to all the moms out there!), start with an audio Bible when you're getting ready in the morning, driving to work, or even folding laundry.

Step 3: Meditate on the Word. This can look different for different people. Try some things and see what works for you. You may want to find a quiet place, pick a scripture, read it over and over, memorize it, visualize it, pray it, and ask God to speak to you about it.

Or you may want to try the SOAP method. If you're unfamiliar with this, SOAP is an acronym for scripture, observation, application, prayer. Pick some scripture, read it, and see what you initially observe. Is there a command in it? What is the overall message? Have you heard it before? Now think about how you can apply the scripture to your life. Next take it to God. Pray and ask God to show you more about this verse, how it applies to you and your life, and if He wants to tell you anything more about it.

I would recommend journaling after you meditate on the Word so you can return to it and see how God's been speaking to you and working in your life. Again, try a few things and see which method you prefer. It doesn't have to be what I've included here, just whatever works for you to really meditate on scripture.

Step 4: Do it! Don't just read the Word. Be a doer of the Word. James writes,

> But don't just listen to God's word. You must do what it says. Otherwise, you are only fooling yourselves. (James 1:22 NLT)

Get the Word in your heart and then do it. And pray throughout your day to consult with God on what you are doing and saying; He's with you and He cares about your life. Even the mundane details that you wouldn't want to "bother" Him with. Trust me: He cares. When one of my kids asks me to help them zip up a jacket, I help them. It's a mundane thing, nothing out of the ordinary. I may use it as an opportunity to get them to try it themselves and coach them as they do, but the point is I don't just leave them alone to fend for themselves. I walk alongside them in their day-to-day tasks and activities. We are God's children. He wants to walk alongside us in our day-to-day lives too.

Step 5: Find a church. If you don't currently have a home church, of all the steps, this is probably the most intimidating. But here's the thing: God created us for community. Yes, scripture says that we are the church and some people use that as an excuse not to attend a local church. But the Bible also says in Genesis 2:18 (NLT), "It is not good for the man to be alone." Jesus had twelve disciples that He kept close. If we weren't meant to be in community, He probably would have just written the Bible Himself and left. God created us for community. We need people to pray for us, walk alongside us, keep us accountable, cry with us, and celebrate with us. So if you aren't already part of a local church, *please* find one. Pray about it and go to a few different ones if you have to, but find one that works for you and then call it home.

These steps will help you grow in your relationship with God and start to become more sensitive to the leading of the Holy Spirit. The Bible says,

> Don't worry about anything; instead, pray about everything. Tell God what you need, and thank him for all he has done. Then you will experience God's peace, which exceeds anything we can understand. His peace will guard your hearts and minds as you live in Christ Jesus. (Philippians 4:6–7 NLT)

He wants to be first in our lives. He wants us to consult Him throughout our day. He wants us to be led by His Spirit. Jesus even said,

> But I tell you the truth, it is to your advantage that I go away; for if I do not go away, the Helper (Comforter, Advocate, Intercessor—Counselor, Strengthener, Standby) will not come to you; but if I go, I will send Him (the Holy Spirit) to you [to be in close fellowship with you]. (John 16:7 AMP)

The more you do these things, the more natural it will all become. You will start hearing God's voice throughout your day—a prompting to talk to someone, a feeling to avoid going somewhere, little things that will have a huge impact on your life and potentially the lives of others. And as we have been talking about, when you have God's voice in your head, it silences the negative self-talk and negative thoughts. We become more aware of who we are in Christ and begin to walk in that knowledge. *Self-love really comes from knowing and loving God.*

Reflection/Discussion Questions

- Have you ever questioned why God made you the way He did?
- What do you believe about God's character, and how does that affect how you see yourself?
- Do you have a hard time moving head knowledge to heart knowledge?
- Do you ever let your emotions/feelings into the driver's seat of your life?
- Do you let the Holy Spirit lead your day-to-day life?
- Which of the five steps listed at the end of the chapter stands out to you the most and why?

Chapter 4

SATAN'S NOT-SO-SECRET WEAPON

Like. Share. Repeat.

If we are truly going to learn to love ourselves, we have to talk about social media. More specifically, let's talk about the inevitable side effect of social media: comparison. Comparison, in my opinion, is public enemy number one when it comes to self-love.

When it comes to comparison, social media is king. And like it or not, we have all become loyal subjects. We live in a social world; that's our reality. Unfortunately that reality comes with endless opportunities to succumb to the cutthroat kingdom of comparison. You might be thinking, *What in the world is she talking about?* and that's a completely fair question. Let me explain.

Social media is an incredible tool, but it is both a blessing and a curse. I don't know a single person who is active on social media and has complete 100 percent peace about it. What I mean by that is that even if you only have social media to post positive messages and scriptures, even if you only follow other accounts and don't make your own posts, even if you have the very best of intentions, constantly scrolling through the highlight reels and filters of other people's lives drags us into the inevitable trap of comparison.

You may think that comparison isn't such a bad thing. In fact, maybe you find it motivating to see how other people look, what they've accomplished, where they are traveling, etc. And I agree it can be motivating now and then. However, when we are constantly bombarded with it, it becomes less of "I am so happy for that person and where they are at in life—good for them" and more of "I wish I were at that point in my life" and even "Why am I not at that point in my life?" Social media comparison can lead to depression, envy, eating disorders, infidelity, divorce, substance abuse, and more. I realize that sounds excessive, but it's true.

There are studies on the effects of social media on teenagers, mental health, and marriages because social media has become a pillar in our lives, but the foundation beneath the pillar is cracked. According to McLean Hospital, the largest psychiatric affiliate of Harvard Medical School and a world leader in mental health care and research, using social media activates the brain's reward center by releasing dopamine. Dopamine is a feel-good chemical that is linked to pleasurable activities such as sex, food, and social interaction. Social platforms are purposefully designed to be addictive and are associated with anxiety, depression, and even physical ailments.[2]

Throughout my life, I never saw myself as good enough because I was constantly comparing myself to others. I'm not as funny as her, as skinny as her, as pretty as her, etc. I compared everything about myself to others. And unsurprisingly, I never measured up.

So how do we rise above being bombarded with opportunities to compare ourselves to others twenty-four/seven?

We have unlimited access to everyone's highlight reels and that can make it hard to love yourself. Why? Because we are humans and love to compare things; it's in our nature. Seriously, it started all the way back with Adam and Eve! The serpent tempted Eve by getting her to compare herself to God. Take a minute to actually stop and think about it. He told her that if she ate the fruit, she would be like God. That inevitably led Eve to compare herself to God. He can do this and I can't … but could I? He knows this and I don't … but could I? Comparison: Satan's not-so-secret weapon.

---

[2] https://www.mcleanhospital.org/essential/it-or-not-social-medias-affecting-your-mental-health.

Hard to Love

We compare our clothes to their clothes. We compare our cars to their cars. We compare marriages, kids, vacations, houses, even pets! We compare everything. We might not even know we're doing it. What is so easy to forget is that most people posting on social media are posting their absolute best—what they want people to see, what they want people to envy, what they want people to believe about them. They also post what will get them those likes (been there, done that). That's the honest truth. If you say that people liking your post has never crossed your mind, I would be willing to bet that you are not only lying to me but to yourself. I am not a social media influencer—far from it. I am very selective of who I allow to follow me because I'm a very private person. But even then, if I post a picture of my kids and it only gets ten likes, I get upset! *My kids are adorable! How dare you not validate that to me and the rest of my followers/friends by double tapping this picture of them that you probably didn't even see or scrolled past in a blur.* It's completely nonsensical, but social media can have that effect on us.

I want to say that because I'm fully aware of how harmful comparing ourselves to others can be that I'm above it all, but I'm not. I have to constantly check myself. For me, someone who spent the majority of my life with very low self-esteem, I came to the realization a while back that I needed to make some changes regarding my social media because it can be a very slippery slope. I used to follow a lot of fitness accounts because I enjoy working out and I'm always looking for new exercises and workouts to challenge myself. Nothing wrong with that, right? Well, I found that the accounts I originally started following to motivate me were actually doing the opposite. I found that I was comparing myself to the fitness models and gym gurus. It started with envying their fitness levels, how they looked, etc. Then I started to feel down about myself because I didn't look like them. Why didn't I look that good? Those thoughts led to the thinking, *Well if my only job was to be in shape and look good, I could look like that too.* Wow. It sounds like Bitter Betty and Jealous Judy joined my pity party, doesn't it? That's not healthy and that's not how I want to live my life. I work out because I like feeling strong, I like being fit, and I want to set a healthy example for my kids. But if I'm going to start comparing myself to everyone in the fitness industry, I am allowing myself to become a body first and a person second *again*. And I can't do that; I won't do that. It honestly started taking away any joy and release I found in exercise and made it feel like a chore.

So I made some changes. I unfollowed a lot of accounts, and honestly it felt *soooooo* good. It took some hard truths to realize what sort of stuff triggered me and what was unhealthy for me personally. Once I did it though, once I clicked those unfollow buttons, it made my social media so much more positive. Don't get me wrong. It didn't get rid of all the comparisons, but seeing my friends on vacation, doing fun and creative things with their kids, I've found that I am able to manage those comparisons without unfollowing them by constantly checking myself and being aware of what I'm doing. Self-awareness is a skill that can be practiced and can change your life drastically.

Let's look at that a bit more: self-awareness. One habit that I became painfully self-aware of on my journey to self-love was my internal dialogue. Now before I delve into that, I was recently informed that not everyone has an internal dialogue and that fact *blew my mind!* Can you believe that? If you are one of those people who does not have an internal dialogue, please reach out to me and let me know what your day-to-day life is like because I imagine it to be so peaceful and I will continue to believe that until you let me know otherwise. That said, the majority of us do have an internal dialogue and we need to pay attention to it.

Would you walk into a store, march up to someone, and say, "Hi. You're useless. You're fat and you never do anything right. No one wants to be around you. No one loves you. You're a failure and you'll never amount to anything"? If you would, put down this book, Google therapists in your area, and make an appointment immediately! Seriously though, what I'm trying to say is that we wouldn't walk up to a stranger, never mind someone we love, and say those incredibly hurtful things. So why do we say those things to ourselves?

First things first, we need to figure out who we really are. The best way to do this is by diving into scripture. Reading our Bibles is also one of the most important things we can do for our self-esteem. When we discover what God says about us in scripture, it can change our perspective on ourselves. And remember that God doesn't lie. He's incapable of it, so if He says something about you, you had better believe it. I understand that sometimes that is easier said than done but, at the very least, you need to work at trying to believe it and receive it. These scriptures are important tools (even weapons) for when we are tempted to compare or when we are feeling down about ourselves. We can remind ourselves who we are and whose we are. As children of God, nothing can take that away from us.

Here are a few of the things God says about you; feel free to look these up in whatever Bible translation you prefer, although I recommend New International Version:

> You are forgiven (Psalm 103:2–3).
>
> You are God's workmanship (Ephesians 2:10).
>
> You are loved (John 3:16).
>
> You are a new creation in Christ (2 Corinthians 5:17).
>
> You are alive with Christ (Ephesians 2:5).
>
> You are worth dying for (Romans 5:6–8).
>
> You are cared for (Philippians 4:19).
>
> You have received abundant grace and the gift of righteousness (Romans 5:17).

You are the light of the world (Matthew 5:14).

You are a joint-heir with Christ (Romans 8:17).

You are valuable (1 Corinthians 6:2).

You are the righteousness of God (2 Corinthians 5:21).

You are strong (2 Timothy 1:7).

You are holy and blameless before Him in love (Ephesians 1:4; 1 Peter 1:16).

You have the mind of Christ (1 Corinthians 2:16; Philippians 2:5).

You are protected (Psalm 121:3).

You have the peace of God that surpasses all understanding (Philippians 4:7).

You have the Spirit of God living in you and He is greater than the enemy in the world (1 John 4:4).

You are more than a conqueror through Him who loves you (Romans 8:37).

You can do whatever you need to do and face whatever you need to face in life through Christ Jesus who gives you strength (Philippians 4:13).

You are chosen by God (1 Peter 2:9).

You are born again—spiritually transformed, renewed and set apart for God's purpose (1 Peter 1:23).

You have authority and power over the enemy in this world (Mark 16:17–18; Luke 10:17–19).

Hard to Love

Your body is a temple of the Holy Spirit (1 Corinthians 6:19).

You are the head and not the tail (Deuteronomy 28:13).

You are redeemed (Galatians 3:13).

You are a citizen of heaven (Philippians 3:20).

You are chosen (Romans 8:33, Colossians 3:12).

You are unique (Psalm 139:13).

You belong to God (1 Corinthians 6:20).

You are an important part of Christ's Body (1 Corinthians 12:27).

You are adopted as His child (Ephesians 1:5).

You have been justified (Romans 5:1).

You are Christ's friend (John 15:15).

You are made in God's image (Genesis 1:27).

If you made it through that entire list, I hope you're feeling good about what your Creator says about you. Also, that list is by no means exhaustive. The Bible says so many things about us, as God's children, so please keep exploring the Word for yourself. After all, it's God's love story to us. It's how he tells us who He made us to be. Take some time and read over that list again. It's pretty incredible, isn't it?

I recently bought my daughter a book for Christmas that has some of these "things God says about me" in it. I want her to know who she is in Christ Jesus and it's what He says about her that matters, not the rest of the world. Especially when I know how harsh and cruel the world can be.

This next little anecdote breaks my heart, even recounting it again now. One night a little while ago, my sweet daughter started crying in her room. When I asked her why she was crying, she told me that she had taken off her princess dress (she was playing dress up with Disney princess dresses just before that) and now she wasn't beautiful anymore. My heart instantly shattered into a million pieces and my eyes welled up with tears. How could this perfect little five-year-old girl think she wasn't beautiful? *Five years old!* How had the enemy gotten into her ear so young? So as much as I wanted to cry in that moment for feeling like a failure as a parent, for not somehow preventing this, for the fear in my heart because I don't want her to struggle with this all of her life just like I did, I sat with her and I held her while she sobbed. I told her that she is absolutely beautiful inside and out. I told her that clothes are clothes and clothes aren't what make a person beautiful. What makes her beautiful is that God created her and *He* made her beautiful. What makes her beautiful is the kind and loving spirit inside of her at such a young age. What makes her beautiful is that Jesus died for her.

After she stopped crying, we got up and I forced her to do the affirmations she has on her bedroom wall. She fought me a bit before agreeing to do them, but once she did, she had a smile on her face. These are in a picture frame on her wall with half a rainbow on either side of them.

> I am strong.
> I am brave.
> I am smart.
> I am unique.
> I am kind.
> I am loved.
> I am beautiful.
> I am honest.
> I am enough.

We now do these each night (or morning, depending on the day)

Hard to Love

and she even reminds me if I forget. And by the time we get to the end, she's shouting the final few. She loves it! Our words have power, whether we are speaking to other people or to ourselves.

When we label ourselves or when we allow others to label us, it impairs our ability to love. Have you ever put a sticker on something and then tried to take it off—especially after a long period of time—and that gross, sticky residue is left behind? Life can be like that. When someone labels us or puts a label on our lives, it can be hard to fully remove. You're fat. You're ugly. You're worthless. You're no good. You're never going to be anything. And eventually another sticker or label gets put over top of that one, and another, and another. Even if we try to take them off, some of that sticky residue can remain. Sometimes we don't even notice it's still on us until someone else comes into our life, gets close to us, and some of that residue rubs off on to them.

It's hard because we live our lives with people and people are imperfect. They hurt us and we hurt them. I guess what I'm trying to say is that it's OK to have feelings and be upset when someone hurts those feelings. But if you let those feelings dictate everything you do and decide who you become, that's when you get into the danger zone. Yes, we should have friends and people close to us but the most important relationship in our lives should be our relationship with Jesus. His words are more important than what anyone else says to us or about us.

Maybe you've been through a lot. Maybe someone spread rumors about you. Maybe they bashed you online and you feel like your life is over. Maybe you're trying everything you can to fit into a certain crowd even though you know you aren't being true to who you really are. Maybe you really care what people think so you go to great lengths to please everyone around you. Maybe you have an approval addiction.

I myself am a recovering approval addict, and I can tell you that life is much better with an audience of one—as long as that one is God! There's a quote from Dennis Rodman (Go Bulls!) that

I loved as a teenager. "Don't let what other people think decide who you are." I loved that quote and clung to that quote like nobody's business. See, Dennis Rodman was different from all the other NBA players I loved to watch. He was different (some people back then would probably choose to say "weird" over "different"), but he was still thriving, at the top of his game. He was one of the *unstoppabulls!* He was one of my favorite players because I admired his skill—rebounding and defense—but also his unapologetic uniqueness. And that quote was an attitude that I desperately wanted to embody myself. But it took me a long time and a lot of work on myself to get to the place where I could finally say that the quote I loved as a kid (and actually used as my yearbook quote) finally means something in my life. Through some not so enjoyable experiences, which we'll get into later, I finally stopped letting other people decide who I was. How did I do it? By finally and truly letting what Jesus did for me on the cross define me and who I am today.

Does Jesus define your life? Or is it friends? Family? Lovers? Work? Experiences? Travel? Fashion? What defines you, and how is it working for you so far?

I'm going to give you some homework now (sorry, not sorry). I want you to stand in front of a mirror and say some of the things from the list in this chapter (the long list with scriptures). Pick three or four to start with and personalize them by saying, "I am God's workmanship" and "I am loved." Do this and see how you feel after. If you're someone who journals, do this exercise and then sit down to journal what you experienced. Is it hard to say those things about yourself, or does it come easily? How does it make you feel? If it's hard (it used to be for me too, so you are not alone), keep doing it. Do it each morning and eventually the words will take root. God's Word can transform our hearts! Even if saying those things comes easily to you, keep doing it. It's such a healthy habit to build into your routine, and knowing who you are in Christ will change your life!

Reflection/Discussion Questions

- What purpose or role does social media have in your life?
- Have you ever compared yourself or your life to something you've seen on social media?
- Do you follow any social media accounts that tend to trigger your comparison more than others? If so, are you willing to unfollow them?
- How would you describe your internal dialogue?
- How did you feel after reading the list of things that God says about you?
- Has anyone ever put a label on you? Is there still some sticky reside left over from it?

Chapter 5
EMBRACE ALL OF YOU

Embrace your weird. Embrace your mistakes. Embrace all of who God made you to be.

Part of my journey to loving myself has been coming to terms with the fact that I'm different. I'm not the same as everyone else. In fact, no two people are exactly the same. We may have similar interests, thoughts, goals, hobbies, etc., but we are all different. God has made each of us unique and that is what makes us beautiful. If you think of snowflakes—how each one is unique and different—doesn't that completely blow your mind? It blows my mind every time I think about it because where I'm from, we get a lot of snow (seriously, it's too much) so to comprehend that each tiny flake is different and unique ... how unbelievably beautiful is that? Well, we are much more important to God than snowflakes, so you can imagine how much more He must delight in the beauty of our uniqueness, our exclusivity.

You are the only you, and I am the only me. I'm going to strive to be the best me I can be, and you should strive to be the best you that you can be. It's a simple concept, right? But in a world ruled by comparison, it's a lot harder than it sounds. If we aren't careful, we can spend our entire lives trying to be someone else.

Growing up I had a hard time finding my identity. I attached myself to a lot of things, I changed who I was for certain people, I tried to belong to different groups of people ... I struggled to just be me. The biggest driving factor behind this was the fact that I didn't love myself so I tried to be anything and anyone else. It took me thirty-plus years, but hey, I can finally say that I love myself! Is it still a struggle at times? Yes. Do I still compare myself to others sometimes? Yes. Am I perfect? Ha! We all know the answer to that.

I was driving around the other day, listening to my local Christian radio station, and heard something that I had to write down. It was one of the only times that this particular station didn't play music, and usually during these times, I switch to a throwback station and jam to some hits from the 1990s and 2000s. But this time, for some reason, I didn't switch. It sounded like an old school sermon—you know the kind. It had echoey acoustics and the second you hear it, you picture a Billy Graham-type scene with a preacher on a stage in a stadium for a revival. You know the visual I'm thinking of. Anyway, I listened for a few minutes and the preacher (whose name I never got because I started listening part way through) said, "Envy and jealousy destroy your ability to love." Wow. Let that sink in for a moment. That hit me hard. I absolutely could not get that sentence out of my head for days after because it really struck my heart. It's such a heavy but truthful statement.

Now when I say the word *comparison*, I think we can all admit, even if it's reluctantly, to having compared ourselves to someone else before. (It's OK. I won't tell.) But words like *envy* and *jealousy* ... those hit differently. The negative connotation attached to those two words is palpable. No one wants to be associated with those two words. Those words are bad and ugly so if they are somehow attached to us, we think that we must be bad and ugly.

But the truth of the matter is that when we compare ourselves to others, more often than not it is cloaked in envy and jealousy. And when we have jealousy and/or envy in our hearts, we can't truly love others. How can we love someone with sincere intentions while secretly coveting what they have, what they do, or how they look? The answer is simple; we can't. If we don't check our hearts for envy and jealousy, we can start to help others and show love to others out of religious obligation. Sometimes we can even start doing it to get something out of it. Both of these scenarios are problematic because we should be helping and loving people from a place of genuine love, mercy, and grace. There's a big difference.

One of my favorite speakers in the world, Paul Scanlon, said, "Others may have your talent, but nobody has your twist," and I absolutely *love* that because it's so true. Grasping that concept also takes the comparison away; other people may be able to do what I do, but they aren't me. I am set apart. I have a purpose. I have a story. I was made by a creative God to be unique, and I need to embrace that. Comparing myself to others and believing I'm less than them is, in fact, admitting that I don't trust God. But I can testify from personal experience that He is worthy of our trust!

> He is the Rock, his works are perfect,
> and all his ways are just.
> A faithful God who does no wrong,
> upright and just is he. (Deuteronomy 32:4 NIV)

Did you catch that? *His works are perfect!* He does no wrong! You are who you are for a reason. He made you the way He made you for a reason. You are not less than the person you compare yourself to. You are you and God loves you where you are, the way you are right now in this moment. Believe it or not, God doesn't have favorites. He doesn't love worship leaders more than the person who cleans the floors. It's just not who God is. He sent Jesus to die for everyone, including you, not just for your pastor.

> Then God said, "Let us make mankind in our image, in our likeness, so that they may rule over the fish in the sea and the birds in the sky, over the livestock and all the wild animals,] and over all the creatures that move along the ground." So God created mankind in his own image, in the image of God he created them; male and female he created them. (Genesis 1:26–27 NLT)

Hard to Love

God made mankind in His image—male and female. He created us. A piece of art doesn't question the artist who created it. It shines brightly and boldly, standing out from the plain walls behind it. We are God's art; embrace it. And let's be real: we all have different tastes in art so it's OK if you're not everyone's "taste," so to speak. It's not your job to impress people. It's your job to be who God created you to be.

I'm going to share a story with you that helped me to grasp this concept of finally being me.

When I first heard Lisa Bevere speak at a women's conference, I was still a fairly new Christian. It is not an exaggeration to say that she completely blew my mind. Her story, her faith, her commanding presence, her confidence, her career, everything about her fascinated me. I wanted to do what she did, speak how she spoke and live like she lived. Oh, how I envied her. I wanted to be her. Over the years, God confirmed to me that He wanted me to write and to speak. You would think that should have been exciting for me, right? I thought it would be too, but after all the mistakes I'd made and all the times I'd messed up, I knew I could never do it. I couldn't do it because after Lisa Bevere got saved she didn't backslide into her old habits and live a sinful life again. She never ran from her calling or from God. Nope. To me, she barely even made mistakes! She stayed a faithful woman of God. And because I had a different story, I knew I couldn't do anything like what she did. The Bible says we are all called but God must have dialed a wrong number when He called me. He must have wanted that for me when I first got saved, but now that I'd messed up so much, things were different. I figured that I had robbed myself of my destiny—becoming the next Lisa Bevere—because of all the mistakes I'd made.

I was jealous of her ability to move forward in her faith and her calling and not struggle with backsliding or things of the past. (Keep in mind that I didn't and don't know her personally and had absolutely no idea what she has struggled with or the ins and outs of her journey, I just had my perception.) After throwing myself a pity party or two, let me tell you what God told me when I finally stopped whining and actually started to listen to Him regarding my calling. He said, "You can't be her because she is already her. You are you. I made you to be you. No one else is like you and no one else has your story. Be you. The only you. Not another her. Be who I created you to be."

It took me a long time to come to terms with all the mistakes I'd made along the way. But when I did, it changed my life! I realized that as much as I loved Lisa Bevere and her teachings (and still do), I had always felt beneath her because I couldn't relate to her in the way that I thought I needed to. I put her on a pedestal, even made her somewhat of an idol, if I'm being honest. But through that, God showed me that if I struggled with what I struggled with, there must be others who struggled too. God knew I would mess up and He still called me. He called me because I know what it's like to feel guilt, shame, and condemnation in the worst ways. I know what it's like to fall back into a life that I was so happy and thankful to get out of when I was first saved. I know what it's like to look in the mirror and want to cry because I failed again. I know what it's like to question my salvation and to wrestle with the fear and attacks of the devil when he won't stop coming. I know. Maybe you know too. You aren't alone, and you aren't without hope. I've been there. I've come through it, and I'm walking tall. So can you!

Back to my favorite speaker (seriously, he's got so much wisdom he shares with the world!), I once heard Paul Scanlon say, "You can never disappoint God. He already knows what you're going to do. It's not a surprise to Him so it can't disappoint Him." Ahh! Isn't that so amazing and refreshing to hear? I feel like I should get this tattooed somewhere! God knew I would mess up as many times as I've messed up, and He knows I'll mess up more. Guess what. He didn't call me to be perfect. If I were perfect, I wouldn't need Jesus, and believe me: I need Jesus desperately each and every day.

Let's look at 1 Corinthians 1:27 (NLT). The Bible says,

Hard to Love

> Instead, God chose things the world considers foolish in order to shame those who think they are wise. And he chose things that are powerless to shame those who are powerful.

I'll never be perfect. Neither will you. If God took a perfect person and did great things with him or her, we wouldn't be that impressed, would we? But when God takes someone who has seen hurt, pain, mistakes, storms, and trials and changes that person for His purpose, now *that* is something we notice and *that* is something that glorifies Him.

Before I could step into my calling though, I needed to deal with my shame. I struggled with shame for more years than I care to admit. Shame is a powerful tool that Satan uses to weigh us down. He doesn't want us to have the freedom that comes with confession. We spend so much time trying to be who we think the church wants us to be and who our Christian friends want us to be—even who *we* think we should be. We're all human. We aren't perfect. Get over it. I'm sorry if that sounds harsh, but I've come to realize that shame only has power if you let it. And if you are consumed by shame, it will absolutely hinder your ability to love yourself, love God, and love others. Why? Because shame prevents you from fully loving and accepting yourself.

If you struggle with shame, ask your home church what programs they offer to help with that. I've been through both Freedom and Celebrate Recovery and both are incredible programs!

Now, let's talk about Peter for a moment. You know, that guy in the Bible, one of Jesus's disciples, church planter—*the* Peter. He's kind of a big deal, right? But before Peter got his ducks in a row, he messed up. Let me clarify, he didn't just mess up once, he messed up quite a few times. You probably already know that he denied Jesus three times after He was taken away to be crucified, but even before that even happened, Peter let Jesus down. Peter promised to be there for Jesus and all Jesus asked him to do was to stay awake in the Garden of Gethsemane. Seems easy enough. But Peter fell asleep not once, not twice, but three times! Personally, that is something that I can relate to. God tells us to do something and we say we will. Then the distractions trickle in and we end up falling asleep (literally or metaphorically speaking) and not doing what God's asked us to do. I've personally fallen asleep more than three times and I think it's safe to say that most of us have. After the crucifixion and resurrection though, Peter got his act together. He marched forward, and by Acts, he was doing amazing things for the gospel. If Peter can do it, so can we!

Knowing and accepting what you've done, and moving on from that—even if you have to do it daily—is important. Knowing yourself and knowing God on an intimate level is even more important. We all have behaviors, attitudes, and fears that we've learned over time, and recognizing and understanding why we do the things we do is vital to our walk with God. But we can't stop there. Recognizing and understanding why we do things isn't enough. We need to change them. Bad behaviors, attitudes, habits, reactions, all of that stuff that we say, "Well I do that because _____," is stuff that needs to change. We can't make excuses forever. We need to give it over to God—yes, even if it's multiple times a day—and ask Him to change our hearts. He will do His part, but we have to be faithful and pure hearted in our intentions on our side of things too.

I used to be incredibly defensive. You could be trying to help me by telling me that there was a tiny bit of chocolate on my face and I would assume that you were calling me fat and ugly. I realize that's completely irrational, but that's seriously how offendable and defensive I used to be. I thought everyone was out to get me. If you told me that maybe a semicolon would be better than a comma in one of my school reports, I went on the attack and defended that comma as if it were my own flesh and blood! It was a problem. My low self-esteem trained my mind to react that way. I couldn't accept that someone was genuinely trying to help me because I didn't feel worthy of that. I assumed everyone was putting me down in every way they could. When I continued to turn to alcohol to drown my feelings and pain, I realized that I truly had a problem. And when I figured out why I continued to seek refuge in the arms of men instead of the arms of God, I thought, *I've figured it out so now I'm free!* I assumed that since I'd figured it out, I wouldn't repeat my mistakes and all would be well in my life. Is that how things actually went? Nope. Truthfully, it didn't give me any sort of freedom from the issue; it just gave me an excuse to keep doing what I was doing. I used that as a justification to continue living exactly how I always had. I justified it because of what I'd been through and what I'd been programmed to believe.

The point of that little ramble is that it's not enough to know your character flaws and why you do what you do. You need to work on them with a genuine desire to do better, and you need God's grace to do it. It won't be easy at first, but as with a lot of things that require hard work, it is absolutely worth it. Remember that what was done *to* you (whatever has programmed these behaviors in you) does not dictate who you are. What was done *for* you does that. Jesus died for you so that you could be free from all of that.

No matter what you've been through, what you haven't been through, what you're afraid to go through, what you've put other people through, someone else on this planet can relate to you. Knowing that can mean the world when you're feeling alone.

God is always with us, and we should always turn to Him with problems, cares, and worries, but it also helps to know that there are people on this planet—flawed humans just like you and me—who understand or have similar experiences. Your story is important. It is relevant to you and to others. Your first twenty chapters may be a horror story, an erotic romance novel, or even a complete mystery, but you can write the remaining chapters as a beautiful love story between you and God. It's never too late to start a new chapter.

That new chapter often starts with awareness. We all have different things that we need to be aware of and we have some of the same things that we are already aware of. We all need to be aware that Satan will guide our thoughts to whatever makes us the most insecure, to what tempts us the most, to things we've given up and miss, to whatever he thinks will pull us a millimeter farther from God. You also need to be aware that you have authority over him in the name of Jesus! I know that sounds like another Christian cliché, but it is absolutely true and you need to believe that with all of your heart. We can take the necessary steps to change our thoughts and actions if we are aware of them.

Things that you need to change will differ depending on your background and experiences. If you have struggled with drinking, don't keep alcohol (or other similar substances) in the house. Or if you have trouble with porn or sex outside of marriage, check your social media and unfollow any hypersexual or tempting accounts and don't watch TV shows or movies with graphic sex scenes. Be smart. Don't go to Vegas for a bachelor or bachelorette party if you aren't 110 percent positive that you can withstand the temptations. Don't spend a lot of time (sometimes don't spend any time at all) with people who you partied with, an ex-girlfriend or ex-boyfriend, someone you used to hook up with, etc. Just don't do it. Other addictions apply! Know your weaknesses: codependency, negative self-talk, sarcasm, drugs, low self-esteem, etc. Be smart. Be aware. Figure out your triggers. Know yourself and work on what you know. Ask God to reveal what you don't know so that you can keep growing in your relationship with Him and get one step closer to being who He created you to be.

I'm going to say this again because it's worth repeating: you can't truly know yourself until you know the One who created you. And your relationship with God is like any other relationship. You need to make time for it, put effort into it, communicate, and overcome hurdles for it to flourish. Develop trust for each other and invest in each other, which God has already done through Jesus. Good relationships aren't one-sided either. You need to talk to God, but you also need to take time to listen. It's amazing the things that will happen when you fully trust God!

Hard to Love

I've messed up more times than I can count for more years than I can remember. If God can bring me through that and use it all to help other people, just imagine what He can do with you!

> Jesus looked at them intently and said, "Humanly speaking, it is impossible. But with God everything is possible." (Matthew 19:26 NLT)

I recently heard a song by Josiah Queen called "Fishes and Loaves," and it really struck a chord in my heart (musical pun not intended). He sings the song from the perspective of the young boy who gave his fish and bread to Jesus. Jesus then used them to perform a well-known miracle: feeding thousands of people from just one boy's lunch. (You can read about it in John 6.) The reason this song has been on repeat for me is because every time I hear it, it reminds me that I'm not the one who needs to be perfect and I'm not the one saving the world. That's Jesus. I give Him what I have, which at times doesn't feel like much. But I'm sure in a crowd of thousands, that boy didn't feel like he had enough or that he was enough to make a difference either. *But God.* When we give what we have to Jesus, He does incredible things because He is an incredible God! You don't have to be perfect; you just need to give Him what you have—your heart, your time, your talents—and He can and will do amazing things with them! As the lyrics is the song say,

> Oh I'm tryna to let go
> My heart is uneasy, I give you control
> I know it's not much but I know what I owe
> I'll give you all of my fishes and loaves. (Josiah Queen, "Fishes and Loaves")

Now I have a challenge for you. Take five minutes today and meditate on the scriptures below:

Rather, it should be that of your inner self, the unfading beauty of a gentle and quiet spirit, which is of great worth in God's sight. (1 Peter 3:4 NIV)

For we are God's handiwork, created in Christ Jesus to do good works, which God prepared in advance for us to do. (Ephesians 2:10 NIV)

You have unfading beauty in you. Recognize that. God put it in you. You are God's handiwork. Who are you to question the Creator's masterpiece? Remember who you are in Christ, meditate on these scriptures today, and come back tomorrow with an open heart. This is going to be a journey!

Reflection/Discussion Questions

- Do you believe that while others may have your talent, nobody else has your twist?
- Do you feel like you are living how God created you to live?
- Have you ever wanted to be someone else or have a different life altogether?
- Have you ever struggled with shame?
- Have you ever gotten distracted or "fallen asleep" when God's asked you to do something?
- Do you have any triggers or anything that is pulling you away from God that you need to be more aware and mindful of?
- Do you put time and effort into your relationship with God?

Part 2
LOVE GOD

Chapter 6
WITH ALL YOUR HEART

> Love the Lord your God **with all your heart**, and with all your soul (life), and with all your mind (thought, understanding), and with all your strength.
> —*Mark 12:30 (AMP, emphasis mine)*

This scripture may sound familiar. Even if you haven't heard it preached on, which I'm confident you have, you must have read it in your Bible or heard it mentioned by another Christian or maybe even seen it on a T-shirt. If you have read it in your Bible, you might have also noticed that it's not just in one place in your Bible. Something I've learned over the years is that nothing is in the Bible without reason and if something is repeated, pay attention!

> Love the Lord your God with all your heart and with all your soul and with all your strength. (Deuteronomy 6:5 NIV)

> The man answered, "'You must love the Lord your God with all your heart, all your soul, all your strength, and all your mind.' And, 'Love your neighbor as yourself.'" (Luke 10:27 NLT)

> "Teacher, which is the most important commandment in the law of Moses?"

> Jesus replied, "You must love the Lord your God with all your heart, all your soul, and all your mind." (Matthew 22:36–37 NLT)

As I said, if you haven't heard this preached on before, there are many sermons and books out there that break down the different parts of this verse. For the purpose of this book and subject matter we are undertaking, I am choosing to share with you my thoughts and what I believe the Holy Spirit has led me to share with you. So while there may be different opinions and interpretations of this particular scripture out there, this is what God has put on my heart for you.

Before we get into how we are to love God, we need to remember that God *is* love. So when God talks about love, when we read anything about love in the scriptures, we know it is straight from God's heart. When He gives us instructions on how to love, we need to take notes.

The Bible tells us in Mark to "love the Lord your God with all your heart, and with all your soul (life), and with all your mind (thought, understanding), and with all your strength" (Mark 12:30 AMP).

I absolutely love the Amplified Version of this verse. It gives us just a little bit extra, and hey, I'm a little bit extra. What can I say? (Just ask my Starbucks barista!)

When I think of loving God with all my heart, I can't help but think of David. I mean seriously, how can I not? He is described in the Bible as a man after God's own heart. Can you imagine that description being part of your legacy? David loved and trusted God with all his heart. We can see it over and over in the book of Psalms. But before we dive into that, let's look at his life prior to him writing the psalms.

Before David was king of Israel, he was a shepherd boy, the youngest of eight brothers. Imagine that grocery bill! Well, God sends Samuel to find and anoint the next king of Israel—God's chosen king. God says to the current king, Saul (terrible king, by the way),

> But now your kingdom shall not continue. The Lord has sought for Himself a man after His own heart, and the Lord has commanded him to be commander over His people, because you have not kept what the Lord commanded you. (1 Samuel 13:14 NKJV)

Samuel traveled to meet Jesse as God told him that's where he'd find the "man after His own heart." Jesse presented seven of his strong, tall, handsome sons to Samuel, confident that the chosen king was among them. But as each son was presented to Samuel, as much as Samuel thought each one looked the part, God said, "Next!" As it turns out, God wanted more. We see it here in verse 7:

> But the Lord said to Samuel, "Don't judge by his appearance or height, for I have rejected him. The Lord doesn't see things the way you see them. People judge by outward appearance, but the Lord looks at the heart." (1 Samuel 16:7 NLT)

David wasn't initially presented to Samuel because he was out tending to the animals (sheep and goats) as a good shepherd does. But when Jesse called for David, he came to meet them, and the Lord said, "This is the one; anoint him" (1 Samuel 16:12 NLT).

So Samuel did as the Lord commanded. These scriptures show us the kind of boy that David was and the kind of man he would grow into. At the time he wasn't as strong in stature as his big brothers, but that didn't matter to God. It was David's heart and faith that made him strong and worthy to be king.

As we look at David's life, what else set him apart? Why is David a man after God's own heart? And how can we learn to be the same?

Well, first things first. David was a man of faith. What is faith? Dictionary.com defines faith as confidence or trust in a person or thing; belief that is not based on proof.

So faith is knowing in our heart of hearts that we can trust God. That's faith in a nutshell, and I have to admit that I find it so incredibly beautiful.

I don't think there are many people in our modern world who don't know the ultimate story of faith. Yes, I'm talking about the story of David and Goliath. Even people who have never picked up a Bible or gone to church a day in their lives know the story of the shepherd boy who killed the giant. It's one of my kids' favorite Bible stories and for good reason.

Let's look at this great example of David's faith.

> And David rose early in the morning and left the sheep with a keeper and took the provisions and went, as Jesse had commanded him. And he came to the encampment as the host was going out to the battle line, shouting the war cry. And Israel and the Philistines drew up for battle, army against army. And David left the things in charge of the keeper of the baggage and ran to the ranks and went and greeted his brothers. As he talked with them, behold, the champion, the Philistine of Gath, Goliath by name, came up out of the ranks of the Philistines and spoke the same words as before. And David heard him.
>
> All the men of Israel, when they saw the man, fled from him and were much afraid. And the men of Israel said, "Have you seen this man who has come up? Surely he has come up to defy Israel. And the king will enrich the man who kills him with great riches and will give him his daughter and make his

father's house free in Israel." And David said to the men who stood by him, "What shall be done for the man who kills this Philistine and takes away the reproach from Israel? For who is this uncircumcised Philistine, that he should defy the armies of the living God?" And the people answered him in the same way, "So shall it be done to the man who kills him." (1 Samuel 17:20–27 ESV)

Goliath, the Philistine champion, the giant, had challenged Israel's army to send someone—anyone—to fight him. But the Israelites were scared, and understandably so. This guy was huge and an experienced warrior. Enter David, the shepherd boy. As David was dropping off food to his brothers, he heard about it, and not only was he not afraid, but he was also angry that someone dared to challenge God's people. In verse 26 he says, "For who is this uncircumcised Philistine, that he should defy the armies of the living God?" I love David's attitude here: *How dare this guy challenge God's people!*

When some of the soldiers overheard David talking this way, they told King Saul and the king sent for David. Again, we see David's unwavering faith in his exchange with the king. We all know how the story ends, but I want you to read through the verses below and pay extra attention to the bolded verses (the emphasis is mine) where we really see David's faith shine through.

> "Don't worry about this Philistine," David told Saul. "I'll go fight him!"
>
> "Don't be ridiculous!" Saul replied. "There's no way you can fight this Philistine and possibly win! You're only a boy, and he's been a man of war since his youth."

But David persisted. "I have been taking care of my father's sheep and goats," he said. "When a lion or a bear comes to steal a lamb from the flock, I go after it with a club and rescue the lamb from its mouth. If the animal turns on me, I catch it by the jaw and club it to death. I have done this to both lions and bears, and I'll do it to this pagan Philistine, too, for he has defied the armies of the living God! **The Lord who rescued me from the claws of the lion and the bear will rescue me from this Philistine!**"

Saul finally consented. "All right, go ahead," he said. "And may the Lord be with you!"

Then Saul gave David his own armor—a bronze helmet and a coat of mail. David put it on, strapped the sword over it, and took a step or two to see what it was like, for he had never worn such things before.

"I can't go in these," he protested to Saul. "I'm not used to them." So David took them off again. He picked up five smooth stones from a stream and put them into his shepherd's bag. Then, armed only with his shepherd's staff and sling, he started across the valley to fight the Philistine.

Goliath walked out toward David with his shield bearer ahead of him, sneering in contempt at this ruddy-faced boy. "Am I a dog," he roared at David, "that you come at me with a stick?" And he cursed David by the names of his gods. "Come over here, and I'll give your flesh to the birds and wild animals!" Goliath yelled.

Hard to Love

David replied to the Philistine, "You come to me with sword, spear, and javelin, but **I come to you in the name of the Lord of Heaven's Armies— the God of the armies of Israel, whom you have defied. Today the Lord will conquer you, and I will kill you and cut off your head. And then I will give the dead bodies of your men to the birds and wild animals, and the whole world will know that there is a God in Israel! And everyone assembled here will know that the Lord rescues his people, but not with sword and spear. This is the Lord's battle, and he will give you to us!"**

As Goliath moved closer to attack, **David quickly ran out to meet him.** Reaching into his shepherd's bag and taking out a stone, he hurled it with his sling and hit the Philistine in the forehead. The stone sank in, and Goliath stumbled and fell face down on the ground.

So David triumphed over the Philistine with only a sling and a stone, for he had no sword. Then David ran over and pulled Goliath's sword from its sheath. David used it to kill him and cut off his head. (1 Samuel 17:32–51 NLT)

Seriously, that story never gets old.
We love God with all of our heart by having faith in who He is.
In verse 37, David recounts what the Lord has already done for him. He remembers God's faithfulness and therefore he doesn't question if He will be faithful again. Even when the king tells him he can't do it, he's not strong enough, and blah blah blah, David doesn't doubt God's ability to use him. Isn't that beautiful? We all face trials and tribulations in our lives, but the silver lining is that

they build our faith. God is faithful. He is good. Even if you haven't faced any Goliath-sized challenges since giving your life to Christ (and you will), the miracle of salvation, the love that God the Father showed by sending His Son to die on a cross for us ... that is what you start building your faith on.

Then we see David speaking his faith out loud. He remembered what God had already done for him, then he spoke words of faith and what he was believing God would do now. We can do those same things.

Next we see David's faith take action. In verse 48, it says that David quickly ran out to meet Goliath. He didn't walk, he ran. His faith in God was so solid that he raced out to meet the Philistine killing machine, knowing that God was with him and that God would bring him victory. That speaks volumes about David's faith.

Let's take a minute to think about this. David remembered what God had already done for him, then he spoke words of faith and what he was believing God for, then he took action. Having faith in God doesn't give us permission to sit around and wait while we twiddle our thumbs. You've undoubtedly heard the expression "Take a step/leap of faith" before. Well, once again, that requires real action. If David had just sat on the battlefield and waited for lightning to strike Goliath, the story might have ended a little bit differently. We need to act in faith, according to God's will. It is for this reason that reading the Bible is so important to our faith. Not only does it provide amazing examples of God's faithfulness, but it also helps us to understand Him and His will.

So let's recap this.

We are called to love God with all our heart.

In order to love God with all our heart, we need to have faith.

In order to build faith, we need to remember all that God's done, believe for what He will do, and act according to His will.

While it may not sound incredibly complicated, you may not really know how to do this or even if this faith building recipe could work for you. Trust me: it can and it's so important that we put in the work to build our faith. When it comes down to it, we should all want to be like David and be men and women after God's own heart!

Later in his life David says,

> I will praise you, Lord, with all my heart;
> I will tell of all the marvelous things you have done.
> (Psalm 9:1 NLT)

David praised God with all of his heart and he spoke of the things God had done. Again, he talks about praising God and His faithfulness, and after reading through the psalms, I have no doubt that this was key to continuing to build his own faith. I'm sure you won't be surprised when I tell you that it can be exponentially helpful to building our faith too.

You might read all of this and think, *Great. I need to be perfect to be a man or woman after God's own heart. I can't be like this David guy.* Well, I have some good news. David wasn't perfect. Yes, he slayed a giant, had incredible faith, and lived for God. David also committed adultery with one of his soldier's wives, got her pregnant, and then had her husband killed to cover up what he'd done. We'll get into this in detail a bit later. It's true that not too many of us have probably faced a physical giant in a miraculous battle (although we've all faced some metaphorical giants, I'm sure). However, I'm willing to bet a lot more of us can relate to David's dirty deeds. Hopefully minus the murder part. I'm talking about sexual sin, shame, trying to keep secrets, hide our wrongs at any cost, and lying about it all. Now that's a relatable dude in my book. Literally. I just called him relatable in my book. Get it? Sorry, sometimes I just can't help myself.

Anyway, my point is that David had weaknesses yet he was, and still is, known as a man after God's own heart. That's encouraging! Don't give up on yourself; pursue God with all your heart. He's worth it!

Reflection/Discussion Questions

- What does faith mean to you?
- Have you ever faced a Goliath-sized challenge?
- What is something God has done for you or brought you through that has helped to build your faith?
- When was the last time you took a step/leap of faith?
- What part of David's life do you relate to the most?

Chapter 7
WITH ALL YOUR SOUL

> Love the Lord your God with all your heart, and **with all your soul (life)**, and with all your mind (thought, understanding), and with all your strength.
> —*Mark 12:30 (AMP³, emphasis mine)*

In the secular world, the term *soul* has become somewhat corrupted. It's thrown around a lot, especially in terms of finding a "soulmate." But if you knew the story behind "soulmates," I don't think people would be so infatuated with it. If you're curious, the story stems from Greek mythology and the gist of it is that Zeus decided to split humans in half because he feared how powerful they might become. After he did this, humans were depressed, lonely, and consumed with despair, missing their other half. They roamed the earth, forever looking for the missing piece of themselves. Essentially, they became broken, empty shells always looking for their other half to make them whole again. And if they didn't find that other half, they were miserable for eternity. How romantic, right? Anyways, that's complete nonsense (and super creepy if you ask me), so let's get to the truth.

The Bible mentions souls repeatedly. In the Old Testament, there are two terms used for *soul:* נֶפֶשׁ *(nephesh)* and ψυχή *(psychē)*. The Hebrew term for *soul* is used over 750 times throughout the Bible.[4]

---

[3] Also see Luke 10:27 (NIV).
[4] https://app.logos.com/tools/factbook?reportId=ref%3Abk.%25soul&title=Soul.

According to scripture, the heart is the center of spiritual activity and of all the operations of human life. Now while "heart" and "soul" are often used interchangeably in our modern world, we can see in Mark 12:30 that this is not accurate. "Heart" and "soul" are mentioned separately so they must be separate entities. The heart is part of the soul.

Your beliefs, will, memory, and emotions make up your soul. And while the soul itself is not a simple concept, I think stating that it is essentially who you are as a person is the simplest way to define it.

When God created Adam's physical being out of dust, it was just that: a physical being. He then breathed life into him.

> And the Lord God formed man of the dust of the ground, and breathed into his nostrils the breath of life; and man became a living soul. (Genesis 2:7 KJV)

According to scripture, our souls make us a living person; our souls are all we are, outside of the physical body we are in. Our minds, our will, our memories, our spirits, our emotions ... all of these things make up our soul. Wow.

When I say the word *soul*, you may have some kind of emotional connection to that term already. And if you don't, maybe you do now after hearing the definition above.

What about when I mention the word *submit* or *submission?* It's certainly possible that you might have a negative connotation come to mind. For me, a mixed martial arts fan, I think of the fights I've seen that were won by submission. One contender wrestles with another to get them into a position so uncomfortable or painful that it forces them to submit or, in the world of fighting, to tap out. The winner is seen as strong and the one who submitted is seen as weak. You may think of a slave submitting to a master or something similar from a movie or show you've seen. No matter what it brings to mind for you, we can probably all agree that the term *submission* is generally not seen as a positive thing. If you'll stick with me here, I want to take a moment to challenge that mentality. In fact, I am going to blatantly state that submission, in terms of submitting ourselves to God, is not a weakness by any means. It's actually the highest form of strength.

So here we are, living in a world where submitting to someone or something is generally a sign of weakness. It means they weren't strong enough to win the fight. I would argue that when it comes to God—as in when we fully submit ourselves to Him—it is the strongest, most courageous thing we could ever do. When we lay it all down and surrender to the One who created it all, it is such a beautiful thing and it is in that place of submission where God's strength shines through us.

The Greek word for *submit* is *hupotassō*, and it means to arrange under, or subordinate; to subject or put into subjection; to subject one's self, or to obey; to submit to one's control; to yield to one's admonition or counsel; to obey or be subject to.

Looking at this, to submit to God means to yield to His advice, to obey Him, and to give Him control. Let's be honest. None of us have it all figured out so we need advice and direction from the only One who does. What does it mean to submit control to God? It's lifting up difficult circumstances to Him in prayer; it's asking for His help; it's talking to Him about our day and listening to hear His voice; it's reading our Bible to deepen our understanding of His will. Let's face it. We need God! Obeying God and submitting to His control may sound hard or even unpleasant (no one likes to be controlled), but God doesn't grab the steering wheel out of hands and just do as He pleases. He chose to give us free will. That means He works *with* us. He wants what's best for us. Even better—He always knows what's best for us. So submitting to God's control isn't as scary as it sounds. It means praying, reading the Bible, doing what the Bible says, and listening to the Holy Spirit, and as Christians, these are all things we should be doing on a daily basis anyway.

In order to love God with all our souls, we need to be willing to submit/surrender everything to Him. Jesus states pretty clearly what we need to do in order to be His followers.

> Then Jesus said to his disciples, "If any of you wants to be my follower, you must give up your own way, take up your cross, and follow me. If you try to hang on to your life, you will lose it. But if you give up your life for my sake, you will save it. And what do you benefit if you gain the whole world but lose your own soul? Is anything worth more than your soul? For the Son of Man will come with his angels in the glory of his Father and will judge all people according to their deeds. And I tell you the truth, some standing here right now will not die before they see the Son of Man coming in his Kingdom." (Matthew 16:24–28 NLT)

We must not hang on to our lives but give up our ways and surrender (submit) to His ways. If we don't, we may gain the world but lose our soul. And then Jesus emphasizes the value of the soul, "Is anything worth more than your soul?" Wow. From God's mouth to our ears.

If you want an absolutely legendary example of fully submitting to God (loving God with all your soul), we have to talk about Mary.

> An Angel Tells about the Birth of Jesus
> One month later God sent the angel Gabriel to the town of Nazareth in Galilee with a message for a virgin named Mary. She was engaged to Joseph from the family of King David. The angel greeted Mary and said, "You are truly blessed! The Lord is with you."

Hard to Love

Mary was confused by the angel's words and wondered what they meant. Then the angel told Mary, "Don't be afraid! God is pleased with you, and you will have a son. His name will be Jesus. He will be great and will be called the Son of God Most High. The Lord God will make him king, as his ancestor David was. He will rule the people of Israel forever, and his kingdom will never end."

Mary asked the angel, "How can this happen? I am not even married!"

The angel answered, "The Holy Spirit will come down to you, and God's power will come over you. So your child will be called the holy Son of God. Your relative Elizabeth is also going to have a son, even though she is old. No one thought she could ever have a baby, but in three months she will have a son. Nothing is impossible for God!"

Mary said, "I am the Lord's servant! Let it happen as you have said." And the angel left her. (Luke 1:26–38 CEV)

So I know we've all heard this story before. Hello! It's the Christmas story. But I need us to pause and look at the sheer magic in these words. First, we need some context. Mary was a young teenage girl who was engaged to be married. She was just about to experience this huge milestone of marriage and, probably soon thereafter, start a family with Joseph. Now back then, having a baby out of wedlock was very frowned upon. It was incredibly shameful and was not a position that any young girl wanted to be in. That is one reason why Mary's response to the angel is so beyond comprehension. "Let it happen as you have said." *What?*

Not only was Mary's future marriage at risk but also her life. Having a child out of wedlock in those days was an offense punishable by death. Not to mention her mental health—the shame she would have faced from all the onlookers. I am amazed every time I read her willingness to jump into it all. But that's Mary. Mary loved the Lord God with all her soul. She submitted every single part of herself to God, including her heart, her mind, her will, her emotions (all making up her soul), and even her body! That's incredible. She submitted to God's will for her life, she trusted Him, and because of that, she carried and raised Jesus, our Savior. Wow.

Another great example of complete submission to God is Abraham.

> Abraham's Faith Tested
> Some time later, God tested Abraham's faith. "Abraham!" God called.
>
> "Yes," he replied. "Here I am."

"Take your son, your only son—yes, Isaac, whom you love so much—and go to the land of Moriah. Go and sacrifice him as a burnt offering on one of the mountains, which I will show you."

> The next morning Abraham got up early. He saddled his donkey and took two of his servants with him, along with his son, Isaac. Then he chopped wood for a fire for a burnt offering and set out for the place God had told him about. On the third day of their journey, Abraham looked up and saw the place in the distance. "Stay here with the donkey," Abraham told the servants. "The boy and I will travel a little farther. We will worship there, and then we will come right back."

> So Abraham placed the wood for the burnt offering on Isaac's shoulders, while he himself carried the fire and the knife. As the two of them walked on together, Isaac turned to Abraham and said, "Father?"
>
> "Yes, my son?" Abraham replied.
>
> "We have the fire and the wood," the boy said, "but where is the sheep for the burnt offering?"

"God will provide a sheep for the burnt offering, my son," Abraham answered. And they both walked on together.

> When they arrived at the place where God had told him to go, Abraham built an altar and arranged the wood on it. Then he tied his son, Isaac, and laid him on the altar on top of the wood. And Abraham picked up the knife to kill his son as a sacrifice. At that moment the angel of the Lord called to him from heaven, "Abraham! Abraham!"
>
> "Yes," Abraham replied. "Here I am!"

"Don't lay a hand on the boy!" the angel said. "Do not hurt him in any way, for now I know that you truly fear God. You have not withheld from me even your son, your only son."

> Then Abraham looked up and saw a ram caught by its horns in a thicket. So he took the ram and sacrificed it as a burnt offering in place of his son. Abraham named the place Yahweh-Yireh (which means "the Lord will provide"). To this day, people still use that name as a proverb: "On the mountain of the Lord it will be provided." (Genesis 22:1–14 NLT)

OK, in my opinion, this story is one of the most intense stories in the Bible. In fact, if I'm honest, I usually skip over this in my kids' bedtime Bible stories. Don't judge me! But seriously, in terms of submitting to God, imagine what Abraham must have been feeling in that moment. His beloved son, the one he waited so long for, and God tells Abraham to sacrifice him. Abraham, being a man who lived fully submitted to the Lord, put aside his thoughts, his emotions (I can't even imagine what he was going through on the inside), his everything, and proved that he was willing to obey God, no matter the cost. How many of us can make that claim about our lives?

Once the angel stops Abraham and the ram appears, he must have felt such relief, but the scriptures don't tell us about that. They tell us that he names the place Yahweh-Yireh, or "The Lord Will Provide." Even under that immense pressure, that seemingly impossible test and the roller coaster of emotions Abraham must have felt, he stays focused on God and names the place Yahweh-Yireh. He didn't name it "The Lord Tested Me" or "The Lord Spared My Son." Abraham remained focused on God in spite of his emotions. He was fully submitted to God's will for his life. Talk about loving the Lord with all your soul ...

So in order to love God with our souls, we need to submit to His will and trust Him with every part of our lives—not just the easy things. Anyone can submit when it's easy. But we are called to be set apart. We are called to obey God even when it's hard and we don't know what's coming next.

Let's pray.

God,

Thank You that You are worthy of my trust. Thank You that You only want what's best for me. If there are areas of my life that I haven't submitted to You, areas where I'm holding back, areas that I'm having trouble giving up control, please show them to me. Please give me the strength to submit every part of my life to You, Lord. In Jesus's name, amen.

Reflection/Discussion Questions

- What do you think of when you hear the word *soul?*
- What comes to mind when you hear the word *submit?*
- What does submitting to God look like in your day-to-day life?
- Looking at the examples of Mary and Abraham, how does that change your perspective of submission?
- Are there any areas of your life that still need to be submitted to God?

Chapter 8
WITH ALL YOUR MIND

> "And you shall love the Lord your God with all your heart, with all your soul, **with all your mind**, and with all your strength." This is the first commandment.
> —Mark 12:30 (NKJV, emphasis mine)

This is the part of the scripture that I always found perplexing. How do I love God with my mind? *What does that even mean?* I was contemplating this while lying in bed the other night—everyone contemplates life and scriptures in bed, *right?* Actually, I was contemplating some family dynamics and it led me to this topic. Stay with me here …

As I was lying in bed, I started thinking about the last few weeks and began to feel convicted about the relationship with a couple of family members. They've been a huge help to us since we had our first child, and they've been a really reliable source of childcare. They love our kids and we truly appreciate them so much. With that said, some time ago, we had an incident where one of them yelled at my son (who was three at the time) and we've had to navigate some, for lack of a better word, *uncomfortable* stuff because of it.

Practically speaking, one of our main sources of childcare was now gone. We felt that the trust had been broken and we needed to rebuild that before entrusting our sweet babies to their care again. From a family dynamics standpoint, we also knew we had to sort some things out so we sat down with one of them to discuss the situation. That talk opened our eyes to some fundamental differences in the way we are choosing to raise our kids and how some family members think our kids should be raised. Needless to say, that was not my (nor my husband's) favorite conversation. It all boiled down to the fact that they don't like tantrums and they don't think they should have to be around them, let alone deal with them.

As I mentioned, this family member yelled at my son when my son was upset (midtantrum), while he was in a corner (making him literally feel cornered), and all of it made him feel terrified on top of every other overwhelming emotion he was experiencing at that moment. The other family member involved had also previously admitted to yelling at my daughter when she wouldn't stop crying because she was upset and missed me while they were babysitting. So we were kind of forced to draw the conclusion that they loved our kids and loved spending time with them just as long as the kids were perfectly behaved. I honestly can't blame them. Kids are hard!

So as we discussed steps moving forward, this family member suggested that we should simply inform our children that they are no longer allowed to have tantrums or get upset when they are with them, at their house, or at any family gathering. Now if you are a parent, you are either laughing hysterically right now or your blood is absolutely boiling. Either response is completely understandable and justified. Telling kids to just not get upset in certain places sounds like a pretty quick fix, right? If only it were that easy!

With my mind running a million miles a minute, I tried to gently explain that toddlers don't have the brain development to regulate or control their feelings and emotions, and even if they did, I still wouldn't tell them that they couldn't get upset around family. I don't want my children thinking that the love these family members have for them is conditional and dependent on their behavior. Not only did I want to protect my kids in this situation, but I also wanted to protect the relationship they had with their extended family members.

While the issue didn't get fully resolved at that time, we decided they could still see the kids, but my husband or I would need to be present and we could all visit as a family. Again, we needed to start rebuilding some trust. Asking someone to partner with you in raising your children is a big deal and—especially for us as first-generation Christians—we need to know that the people in our corner are going to support us as a family and partner with us in how we choose to raise our kids.

After that conversation, I put up a bit of a wall. I told myself that I was protecting my children and that is always my priority, as it should be. But this particular night as I was lying in bed, I started feeling convicted about it all. If I'm being really honest, I realized that I had started acting coldly toward these family members. I wasn't mean, but I also wasn't welcoming when they were around. I didn't go out of my way to reach out to them, and I didn't initiate conversation when we did see them. Like I said, I put up a wall. Please know that I'm not proud of how I acted. Believe me. But that night, as I thought about this, the Holy Spirit spoke to me. See, I knew that I should continue to show love and kindness to them, but I didn't *feel* like it. I was upset and I was protecting my babies, so I told myself it was justified. As such, I didn't *feel* like showing love. That's when the Holy Spirit gently reminded me—He spoke to my heart—that I need to love them in spite of my feelings. And that's when it hit me. I must have experienced a hundred sermons, marriage conference speakers, and books stating that in a marriage, you have to choose to love your spouse each day, even when the butterflies in your stomach disappear. But I'd never heard anyone talk about that concept regarding the other relationships in my life. I started to wonder, *Why not?*

The Bible says we are called to love others. It doesn't say we are called to love others when we feel like it, when we agree on all the same important issues, when our political views align, or when we're getting along swimmingly. (Does anyone actually say "swimmingly" anymore?) It doesn't say that we can shelve our love until we get over our hurt, until they change (or we do), or until we reconcile. It doesn't say any of that. Let's be honest though: life and love it would be a lot easier if it did!

Knowing we are called to love others, even when we don't feel like it, is how we honor and love God with our minds. We do what we *know* we should do, even when we don't *feel* like doing it.

The Bible says that they will know us by our love and that means loving even when we don't feel like it, even when someone feels unlovable, even in the middle of conflict. For my situation, this doesn't mean that I have to trust these family members with my children again right away. I believe that boundaries are very healthy and very necessary in all types of relationships. But it does mean that I can still show warmth, kindness, and love to them as human beings. After all, they too were made in the image of God and *judging them is not my job. Loving them is.* So I can put in effort to repair the trust that was broken. I can show them love and kindness in any situation. I can offer support and grace when the opportunity arises. I can treat them how I would want to be treated. Because no matter how annoyed or angry I am at someone, I need to remember that God loves that person so much that He sent His Son Jesus to die for them. Can you imagine how different the world would be if we all saw each other through that lens?

All this to say that love is a choice and that choice is how we love and honor God with our mind.

Scripture tells us to fix our minds on the things above and to renew our minds.

> Do not conform to the pattern of this world, but be transformed by the renewing of your mind. Then you will be able to test and approve what God's will is—his good, pleasing and perfect will. (Romans 12:2 NIV)

Part of the definition of the word *renew* from Dictionary.com is to "to make effective for an additional period." How perfect is that?

God reminds us to continually renew our minds in order to keep them effective.

How do we renew our minds? One way is by reading our Bible. Another is memorizing and meditating on scripture. Getting God's Word into our hearts helps to redirect our minds to the things of God. Also, being in relationship with and listening to the Holy Spirit is crucial to the renewing of our minds because He can help us to see a holy perspective instead of through the lens of our feelings and experiences (like in my case with my family members). Another way is to simply ask God for wisdom.

> If any of you lacks wisdom, you should ask God,
> who gives generously to all without finding fault,
> and it will be given to you. (James 1:5 NIV)

God's will is for us to love others, and sometimes we need a reminder of that. We need to find ways to focus on the things of God, the things of heaven, and His Holy Word, instead of our fleshly feelings and conflicts. Think about it. Our feelings don't only affect our relationships with people but also can affect our relationship with God. It's easy to have faith and love God when you're seeing miracles left and right, people getting saved, prayers being answered ... You feel His presence and it feels amazing! But what about when God isn't shouting? What about when He's silent? Or His timing is different from yours? When you're facing trials? What about then? Just because you don't feel Him, you don't feel His presence, does that mean He's not there? Just because we don't feel love all the time, does that mean we aren't loved? Of course not! God loves us even when we don't feel it. We can (and should) still show love to those around us, no matter what our feelings are on any given day. Can you imagine if you (or me for that matter) being loved was dependent on someone else's mood? I think we'd all feel pretty unloved most of the time. But thank God that's not how Jesus loves us. His love is unconditional and doesn't waver based on feelings or circumstances. We are called to love in the same way.

Have you ever had a fight with a family member or spouse? Did you get through it? I think it's safe to say that all of us have experienced conflict with a loved one and come through it at some point or another. It would be so much easier to just walk away and cut off everyone who ever hurt us, disagreed with us, challenged us, or had a differing opinion from ours. That would be easy. It would also be very lonely. People are imperfect and therefore will inevitably let us down. But when it comes down to it, with the people we care about, we choose to love them in spite of conflict, differences, and all the messy stuff.

The same goes for loving God and loving others (who aren't close to us). Even when we don't feel like it, we have to stand on our knowledge of scripture and recognize that *we are called to love*. I know I need to love others, even when I'm mad, hurt, etc. My head needs to direct my heart when it comes to those situations. The cliché "Follow your heart" isn't the way to go. It's not biblical. "Follow your heart" is often just a way to justify what you want to do, despite the consequences. Let's be real. The heart doesn't always give wise counsel but it is still involved in our decisions and how we live our lives.

The Bible tells us to guard our hearts for this reason! (See Proverbs 4:23 NIV.) If I had just followed my heart in relationships before meeting my husband, I am certain I'd be a miserable mess today. I say that because in previous relationships, I had feelings. I cared for the other person in the relationship. But that wasn't enough. There was always something off and I knew it in my head, but *the heart wants what it wants*. Well too bad for the heart! Because of the heart, I stayed in unhealthy relationships much longer than I should have. I was used and even abused because of the heart. When I met my husband, my heart, my head, and my spirit all aligned. It's the first relationship that I had ever been in that I could say that. The first relationship that I was head over heels in love (heart), that we didn't have any major issues or deficiencies in our relationship (head), and that I had complete peace when I prayed about it (spirit). I thank God every day for that and for my incredible husband.

If we look to the scriptures, David is an example of following both his fleshly feelings when he clearly knew better and overlooking his feelings to obey God. I love David because his life reminds me that we all make mistakes.

Let's look at 2 Samuel 11.

> Late one afternoon, after his midday rest, David got out of bed and was walking on the roof of the palace. As he looked out over the city, he noticed a woman of unusual beauty taking a bath. He sent someone to find out who she was, and he was told, "She is Bathsheba, the daughter of Eliam and the wife of Uriah the Hittite." Then David sent messengers to get her; and when she came to the palace, he slept with her. She had just completed the purification rites after having her menstrual period. Then she returned home. Later, when Bathsheba discovered that she was pregnant, she sent David a message, saying, "I'm pregnant." (2 Samuel 11:2–5 NLT)

So we see here that David obviously ignored his mind (he knew adultery was wrong) and followed his feelings: lust. Then, as we are about to read, he arranged for Bathsheba's husband to be killed to cover up what he did; he wanted to hide his shame (another feeling).

> So the next morning David wrote a letter to Joab and gave it to Uriah to deliver. The letter instructed Joab, "Station Uriah on the front lines where the battle is fiercest. Then pull back so that he will be killed." So Joab assigned Uriah to a spot close to the city wall where he knew the enemy's strongest men

were fighting. And when the enemy soldiers came out of the city to fight, Uriah the Hittite was killed along with several other Israelite soldiers. (2 Samuel 11:14–17 NLT)

What I can glean from this is that even a man after God's own heart, a man who I honestly believe loved God with everything he had, still made mistakes and was still led astray by his feelings. While our feelings are given to us from God and they have a purpose, they aren't meant to be in the driver's seat. Sometimes our knowledge—our minds—need to overrule or veto our feelings and grab the wheel. I'm not saying it's easy, but I am saying at times it's necessary.

Reflection/Discussion Questions

- Do you find it hard to show love when you don't feel like it? If so, what are some ways that you can show love to others when you don't feel like it?
- Do your feelings ever hop into the driver's seat?
- Is there anyone in your life that you feel convicted to do a better job of showing love to?
- What are some ways you can renew you mind?
- Do you live your life in relationship with the Holy Spirit?
- How do you get God's Word tattooed on your heart?

Chapter 9
WITH ALL YOUR STRENGTH

> Love the Lord your God with all your heart, and with all your soul (life), and with all your mind (thought, understanding), and **with all your strength**.
> —Mark 12:30 (AMP, emphasis mine)

This one is another piece of this scripture that seems to be a bit harder to grasp than loving God with my heart and soul. How do you love God with all your strength? Listen to Christian rap music while I work out? I can do that. But it seems weird that they'd include that in the Bible, right? So there must be more to it.

If you look up the word used for *strength* in this particular verse (Mark 12:30), it's the Greek word *ischus*. Other than sounding a little bit like a five-year-old sneezing, what actually is *ischus*?

Ischus means ability, force, strength, or might.

The word that really sticks out for me here is *ability*. We are to love God with all our ability.

Dictionary.com defines *ability* as "power or capacity to do or act physically, mentally, legally, morally, financially, etc.; competence in an activity or occupation because of one's skill, training, or other qualification."

Essentially our ability is our capacity to do what we do—specifically what we are good at (our competence level at something).

Moving on to the word *might,* Merriam-Webster defines it

as follows: "the power, authority, or resources wielded (as by an individual or group); bodily strength; the power, energy, or intensity of which one is capable."

With those definitions, it becomes clearer that loving God with all our strength means to use our talents (abilities), our authority, and our resources to serve God and His kingdom. That's how I got this concept to click for me. In fact, it actually makes perfect sense!

After reading that, you may be taking mental stock of all your abilities and resources. Maybe you're thinking, *I'm not good at anything! I don't have any money or resources to give! What do I do now?* Well, friend, I can assure you that you do have talents and you do have resources; they just might not be what you think.

Our abilities and talents don't always bring us to full-time ministry, but that doesn't mean we can't serve God with them. Paul addresses this in the verse below. Again, the emphasis included is mine.

> Work willingly at **whatever you do**, as though you were working for the Lord rather than for people. Remember that the Lord will give you an inheritance as your reward, and that the Master you are serving is Christ. (Colossians 3:23–24 NLT)

He doesn't say, "All pastors, all prayer team members, and theology majors serve God in full-time ministry." He says to work willingly at *whatever* you do as if you are working for the Lord. That means anything and everything!

Maybe you're good with your hands and you don't see how that could serve God's kingdom. Use your hands to help with some renovations at church. If you're a mechanic working at an auto body shop, be an honest mechanic. Work without grumbling or complaining—as if you are working for Jesus, not your potty-mouthed, incredibly rude boss who treats everyone poorly. Help a single mom with an oil change ... Do what you can and do it with a humble heart with Jesus at the center.

If you are a stay-at-home mom, raise your kids to know Jesus. Fill your home with love. Put on worship music while you clean and pray while you're cooking. Maybe even cook a meal for a family with a new baby.

We all have something to give toward building the kingdom of God. How do I know that? Because God made each and every one of us and He doesn't make mistakes (shout out to the chapters on self-love). Even if we don't see the value of where we're at and what we're doing, God does. Trust me.

There are some old sayings in the Christian community that I absolutely love and that scare me sometimes too. "People are more likely to read the Christian than the Bible." And another one is "You may be the only Jesus some people see." These sayings carry a healthy dose of reality. People watch us, as Christians, to see how we will act, to see if we are hypocrites, to see if there really is something different about us. That's why it is so important to do whatever we do as if we were doing it for Christ. Because we are ... We are showing the world who He is through what we do and say. And they aren't going to care whether we went to Bible college or not.

In terms of using our abilities and resources, let's look at me as an example. I don't have a degree from a Bible college, but I have a lot of experience going through things that some teenagers go through, including making really bad choices. This experience didn't automatically take me to full-time ministry as a youth pastor. In fact, if I'm being honest, I have never had any desire to become a pastor. However, I do have a desire to help teenagers, and my experience has positioned me to volunteer with youth, share my experiences and learnings with them, and God gave me wisdom to speak into their lives as well. In this example, experience and time were my resources and I used them to serve God and help people.

Another type of resource you might have is financial. I know what you're thinking. *She brought up money. I'm out!* Don't give up on me yet. I have a point. I promise. I want to start by saying that you might not have the financial resources to fund church renovations or outreach activities, and that's OK. Don't get me wrong. It is important that we tithe from what we have, and some people have the resources to give beyond that 10 percent. That's awesome. The kingdom needs those people. That's part of what they are called to do and they are equipped to do it. But not all of us have the money to go above and beyond the tithe. When it comes to giving financially, God cares more about our hearts when we give than the amount we give.

The Widow's Offering

> Jesus sat down opposite the place where the offerings were put and watched the crowd putting their money into the temple treasury. Many rich people threw in large amounts. But a poor widow came and put in two very small copper coins, worth only a few cents.
>
> Calling his disciples to him, Jesus said, "Truly I tell you, this poor widow has put more into the treasury than all the others. They all gave out of their wealth; but she, out of her poverty, put in everything—all she had to live on." (Mark 12:41–44 NIV)

So please don't think that if you don't have hundreds of thousands of dollars to give that disqualifies you from supporting the kingdom financially; it doesn't. The state of your heart when you give is what matters. After all, God loves a cheerful giver!

> Remember this—a farmer who plants only a few seeds will get a small crop. But the one who plants generously will get a generous crop. You must each

decide in your heart how much to give. And don't give reluctantly or in response to pressure. "For God loves a person who gives cheerfully." (2 Corinthians 9:6–7 NLT)

That also applies to our time, our talents, and our experience. Some of us have time that we could volunteer. Time is an incredibly valuable resource. Ask any church and they will agree! The kingdom needs people with all kinds of different resources, not just financial ones. In fact, a resource is defined by Merriam-Webster as "a source of supply or support—an available means." It is whatever you have available to help support the kingdom of God.

I get it. Sometimes we are worn down, worn out, and we feel we don't have any strength or resources left to give. I have been there. Many times. We can get so caught up in giving everything we've got that we forget even God rested on the seventh day! Rest is biblical, and it is holy. We need it. The Sabbath Day is a gift to us from God. It is important to give what we have, but if we allow ourselves to get so burned out and emptied, we won't have anything left to give. So please set boundaries, take care of yourself, and know your limits. Don't feel pressured to say yes to every opportunity that comes your way. I did that when I was first saved. If someone asked me to be on a team, I was going to say yes! After all, if someone at church was asking, it must be an opportunity from God, right? Wrong. Not every opportunity is a divine appointment. Be wise. Use discernment and pray. Get in the habit of saying, "I'll think about it, thanks."

If we stretch our strength too thin, we can't fully use the abilities God gave us. Think about it. If you are gifted in dealing with people and you are on a greeting/host team at church, that's awesome. But if you're also on the sound team and the hospitality/cleaning teams, those teams will take away from your time to connect with others. It will take away a connection that could actually be the reason someone comes back to church and gives Jesus a chance.

> It is useless for you to work so hard
> > from early morning until late at night,
> > anxiously working for food to eat;
> > > for God gives rest to his loved ones. (Psalm 127:2 NLT)

God wants to give us rest so please don't burn yourself out trying to do it all. You have a lot to give, but be wise in how you do it.

Let's go back to that word *ischus* again. It means ability, force, strength, or might.

Force. That's an intriguing word. It often comes with a negative connotation (or a *Star Wars* reference), but what if we're missing the positive side of force?

Dictionary.com defines *force* as follows:

- physical power or strength possessed by a living being;
- strength or power exerted upon a person; physical coercion; violence;
- strength; energy; power; intensity;
- power to influence, affect, or control; efficacious power.

Look at the third and fourth bullets. Strength, energy, influence... Wow. What if part of loving God with all my strength is forcing myself (using my strength, energy, and influence) to do the things that don't always come easy, the things I don't always want to do?

For example, there are some days when I'm beyond tired—I'm talking so exhausted it hurts—and I don't want to read my Bible. Well, I can tell you from experience that, as it turns out, those are the days I need God's Word in my heart the most. But if I don't force myself to do it, I'll miss out on what He has for me. In this sense of the word *ischus*, I see force as forcing myself to develop good habits. I see myself forcing, or pushing, past my flesh, my emotions, my exhaustion, and doing what God has called me to do.

In my opinion, the best way to relate to this is through parenting. If you are a parent, you know that it is exhausting—actually, they need a new word to describe it because *exhausting* just isn't enough! When I had my daughter, she cluster fed for quite some time. This meant that I was only getting fifteen to twenty minutes of sleep at a time. Every. Single. Night. Needless to say, I wasn't at the height of my game, and I was certainly not a pleasant peach to be around. (I'm sure my husband would attempt to disagree, but we both know the truth.) I didn't know how I was going to function the next day or even survive the night, never mind put a smile on my tired face. But I did. Because I had to. Because this child needed me and I didn't have any other choice. I pushed through it all because I knew what I needed to do. I forced myself awake for feeds throughout the night and forced myself to get up and to start my day, take care of my sweet baby girl, and make memories as a family. I don't know how I did it. I just did.

Loving God with our strength is serving God as He has commanded us to. We use our abilities, talents, resources, energy, and influence to further the gospel and build the kingdom. Jesus said,

> "Those who accept my commandments and obey them are the ones who love me. And because they love me, my Father will love them. And I will love them and reveal myself to each of them."
>
> Judas (not Judas Iscariot, but the other disciple with that name) said to him, "Lord, why are you going to reveal yourself only to us and not to the world at large?"
>
> Jesus replied, "All who love me will do what I say. My Father will love them, and we will come and make our home with each of them. Anyone who doesn't love me will not obey me. And remember, my words are not my own. What I am telling you is from the Father who sent me." (John 14:21–24 NLT)

Not just those who accept Jesus's commandments and tattoo them on our hearts; it's those who also *do* them that are the ones who truly love God.

If we look to scripture for an example of someone who loved God with all his strength, I'd have to say Paul would take the trophy. It's not a contest, but if it were ...

Paul (formerly Saul) started out as a Pharisee who sought Jesus's followers to jail or kill them. Sounds like a wonderful guy, right? But oh, how God's love can change someone's heart! Paul had an encounter with Jesus that he couldn't deny, and from that day forward, he was different. After he met Jesus, he loved and followed Christ with all of his heart, soul, mind, and strength. Paul had an advantage in his Christianity. He knew the traditions, the thinking, and the ways for the religious leaders of his day because he used to be one. He was able to use that knowledge and experience to preach the gospel. God used Paul to bring the gentiles into His family, and I think most of us can be eternally grateful for that!

Just look at this!

Paul's Message Comes from Christ

Dear brothers and sisters, I want you to understand that the gospel message I preach is not based on mere human reasoning. I received my message from no human source, and no one taught me. Instead, I received it by direct revelation from Jesus Christ.

You know what I was like when I followed the Jewish religion—how I violently persecuted God's church. I did my best to destroy it. I was far ahead of my fellow Jews in my zeal for the traditions of my ancestors.

> But even before I was born, God chose me and called me by his marvelous grace. Then it pleased him to reveal his Son to me so that I would proclaim the Good News about Jesus to the Gentiles.
>
> When this happened, I did not rush out to consult with any human being. Nor did I go up to Jerusalem to consult with those who were apostles before I was. Instead, I went away into Arabia, and later I returned to the city of Damascus.
>
> Then three years later I went to Jerusalem to get to know Peter, and I stayed with him for fifteen days. The only other apostle I met at that time was James, the Lord's brother. I declare before God that what I am writing to you is not a lie.
>
> After that visit I went north into the provinces of Syria and Cilicia. And still the churches in Christ that are in Judea didn't know me personally. All they knew was that people were saying, "The one who used to persecute us is now preaching the very faith he tried to destroy!" (Galatians 1:11–23 NLT)

Paul's testimony is powerful! It's rooted in his strengths, and he used it to spread the gospel across the world.

Reflection/Discussion Questions

- What abilities do you have that can be used to love God?
- What resources do you have that could help further God's kingdom?
- Who do you have influence over? How can you use that influence to show people who Jesus is?

- Have you heard either of those two sayings before ("People are more likely to read the Christian than the Bible" and "You may be the only Jesus some people see")? What feelings or thoughts do they bring up?
- Have you ever felt burned out from giving too much? Do you have boundaries set to avoid it happening again?

Part 3
LOVE OTHERS

Chapter 10

WHO AND WHY?

I have to start this off with a prayer from my son. I learn so much from my kids and showing love and kindness to others is definitely one of the things they teach me about every day. The other night at dinner, we asked who wanted to pray before we dug in. My son raised his hand and, after thanking God for our food and our family, he prayed, "God, please help the robbers to turn to You, and please show them Your love. Please help them not to do the bad things they used to do. In Jesus's name, amen." And this is not the first time he or his sister has prayed for robbers or criminals either. (They read a lot of superhero stories, hence their concern for robbers). But no matter how many times they pray that prayer, or a similar one, I am still flabbergasted by it every single time. Instead of saying a quick memorized prayer so they can hurry up and eat their mac and cheese, they take the time to pray for people who they know need Jesus. And that kind of love—that pure-hearted love from a child—always brings tears to my eyes.

As a precursor, before we get into our calling to love others and how we can do that, I want to first explicitly state that loving others, including your enemies, doesn't mean that you should not have boundaries. Boundaries are healthy and important. Loving other people does not mean disregarding your own safety or health (both mental and physical). We are not called to be doormats. Some people you might need to love from afar, and that is OK, as long as you have genuine love for them and don't harbor any hate or resentment toward them. Hopefully this will all make more sense as we go through the second half of this book on loving others.

> "Love the Lord your God with all your heart and with all your soul and with all your mind and with all your strength." The second is this: "Love your neighbor as yourself." There is no commandment greater than these. Mark 12:30–31(NIV)

The word *neighbor* has such a friendly ring to it, doesn't it? Think Wilson from *Home Improvement* (I'm really aging myself with that one) or Ned Flanders from *The Simpsons* ("Hidy-ho, neighborinos!"). Neighbors sound friendly and positive. That is, until you've had the incredibly eye-opening experience of a bad neighbor.

Now I absolutely love my neighbors right now (seriously, they are wonderful!), but I've had some bad neighbors in my time. We once had a neighbor who let her giant, untrained dog freely roam the entire neighborhood unattended. She would put him out in their backyard, which should be a normal thing to do, except that their backyard didn't have a fence! So this giant beast came and went as he pleased, roaming around the large community greenspace and into the front yards of everyone on the block. In fact, said dog viciously attacked my dogs on multiple occasions, chased me (which was terrifying to say the least), and did his "business" wherever and whenever nature called. All of this without his owner batting an eye. Not very neighborly in my opinion. Needless to say, we were pretty happy to move after that.

Soon after we did, we discovered our new neighbor liked to spend all day blasting dance music from her outdoor speakers (we actually thought there were raves happening twenty-four/seven next door) while simultaneously dousing herself in tanning oil to spend the entire day baking practically naked in the yard, which unfortunately was the view from my daughter's nursery. To each their own, but having a newborn and being very sleep-deprived at the time, I was not a fan. If she had been blasting throwbacks from the 1990s and 2000s, I probably wouldn't have minded as much, but you get my point. It wasn't very "neighborly" behavior.

The moral of the story is that there are good neighbors and there are not-so-good neighbors. But they are still neighbors.

Now the people mentioned above were my literal neighbors. That said, when the Bible calls us to love our neighbors, God isn't just talking about the people occupying the house, condo, room, or space next to us. No. In fact, when a man asked Jesus this very question, he gave us a clear answer. We need to read Jesus's response to fully understand.

> The Parable of the Good Samaritan
>
> On one occasion an expert in the law stood up to test Jesus. "Teacher," he asked, "what must I do to inherit eternal life?"
>
> "What is written in the Law?" he replied. "How do you read it?"
>
> He answered, "'Love the Lord your God with all your heart and with all your soul and with all your strength and with all your mind'; and, 'Love your neighbor as yourself.'"
>
> "You have answered correctly," Jesus replied. "Do this and you will live."
>
> But he wanted to justify himself, so he asked Jesus, "And who is my neighbor?"
>
> In reply Jesus said: "A man was going down from Jerusalem to Jericho, when he was attacked by

robbers. They stripped him of his clothes, beat him and went away, leaving him half dead. A priest happened to be going down the same road, and when he saw the man, he passed by on the other side. So too, a Levite, when he came to the place and saw him, passed by on the other side. But a Samaritan, as he traveled, came where the man was; and when he saw him, he took pity on him. He went to him and bandaged his wounds, pouring on oil and wine. Then he put the man on his own donkey, brought him to an inn and took care of him. The next day he took out two denarii and gave them to the innkeeper. 'Look after him,' he said, 'and when I return, I will reimburse you for any extra expense you may have.'

"Which of these three do you think was a neighbor to the man who fell into the hands of robbers?"

The expert in the law replied, "The one who had mercy on him."

Jesus told him, "Go and do likewise." (Luke 10:25–37 NIV)

Who helped this man? Was it the priest he saw in the temple on Sunday mornings? Was it a Jewish man like himself? No, it was a Samaritan. It's easy to think that a Samaritan was just someone else who happened down the road that day, but Jesus's illustration was so much more impactful than that. Back in those days, Samaritans were not considered "neighbors" in a friendly sense. They were actually considered closer to enemies.

This is such a powerful parable and we will get more into this story in chapter 7. For our purposes right now, we are looking at the last three verses of the passage where Jesus asks, "Which of these three do you think was a neighbor to the man who fell into the hands of robbers?" The expert in the law replied, "The one who had mercy on him." Jesus told him, "Go and do likewise."

These two men were not physical neighbors. They were from different places; they had never crossed paths previously. Yet Jesus tells us to go and do what the Samaritan man did. In that, Jesus is telling us that everyone we encounter is our neighbor. People are our neighbors, not just the people we live close to, all people. And we are to have mercy on all people, care for them, and show them love, just as the Samaritan did in this parable.

Now that we've established who our neighbor is, why is it important to love our neighbors? Of course, as we just read, Jesus tells us to. That's a good enough reason in itself, but there's more to it than just it being a simple command.

> We love because he first loved us. (1 John 4:19 NIV)

It seems too simple to be true, right? But that is the beauty of it. We love because he first loved us. It's simple yet so profound at the same time. However, if you're like me—a detail-oriented person—here's a bit more for you to sink your teeth into and meditate on. Note that all emphasis in the following scriptures is added by me.

> This is how we know who the children of God are: Anyone who does not do what is right is not God's child, **nor is anyone who does not love their brother and sister.** (1 John 3:10 NIV)

> And this is his command: to believe in the name of his Son, Jesus Christ, and to **love one another as he commanded us.** (1 John 3:23 NIV)

> Above all, **love each other deeply**, because love covers over a multitude of sins. (1 Peter 4:8 NIV)
>
> We know what real love is because Jesus gave up his life for us. So **we also ought to give up our lives for our brothers and sisters.** (1 John 3:16 NLT)
>
> And **do everything with love.** (1 Corinthians 16:14 NLT)

Should I keep going? I could, but I think you probably see where I'm going with this. Scripture is very clear on this subject. There really isn't any gray area when it comes to loving others. We need to do it. End of story.

How do we love others in today's day and age? This is such a valid question because, if I'm being honest, the world is a huge mess. I remember when I first gave my life to Jesus, I had such a passion for people. I literally saw the good in anyone and everyone because I knew they were a child of God and God loved them just as He loved me, which if you've been forgiven a lot, you know the feeling I'm talking about. That fiery passion for people seemed to fade as the years went on. The current state of our world doesn't help either. There is so much hate out there and, as a mother of two young children, I would be happy to build a doomsday shelter in my backyard and protect them from all of it! But seriously, with the world the way it is, it's hard sometimes to be willing to show love to people. There're wars, there's racism, there's hate, there's child abuse, there's human trafficking, there's all of these horrific evils around us, and we are supposed to love through it all. Does God know what a tough ask that is?

Of course He knows. If it were going to be easy, everyone would be doing it. But we are called to be different—to do the hard stuff. Jesus didn't say that the world would know us by how many times we go to church in the week or even by how many people we tell about Him. Jesus said the world would know us by our love. Do the people in your life know you for your love? Do the people in mine? What about the people you only encounter briefly on the street or in a coffee shop? How about the guy that bumped into you and made you spill your coffee this morning? Did you show him love? It's not easy. Trust me. I know. But it is necessary. We need to love because He first loved us. And remember, Christ died for us while we were still sinners so, He also died for the guy who robbed you of your morning caffeine fix. That can be a tough pill to swallow (especially without any coffee to chase it down), but that's the way it is.

If you have ever attended a wedding, chances are you've heard this next excerpt of scripture. It's pretty well-known, even in the secular world, which really goes to show how powerful and beautiful it is. But contrary to how it is commonly used, these scriptures are not about romantic love. These verses are actually about loving others in general (i.e., our neighbors).

Love Is the Greatest

> If I could speak all the languages of earth and of angels, but didn't love others, I would only be a noisy gong or a clanging cymbal. If I had the gift of prophecy, and if I understood all of God's secret plans and possessed all knowledge, and if I had such faith that I could move mountains, but didn't love others, I would be nothing. If I gave everything I have to the poor and even sacrificed my body, I could boast about it; but if I didn't love others, I would have gained nothing.
>
> Love is patient and kind. Love is not jealous or boastful or proud or rude. It does not demand its own way. It is not irritable, and it keeps no record

of being wronged. It does not rejoice about injustice but rejoices whenever the truth wins out. Love never gives up, never loses faith, is always hopeful, and endures through every circumstance.

Prophecy and speaking in unknown languages and special knowledge will become useless. But love will last forever! Now our knowledge is partial and incomplete, and even the gift of prophecy reveals only part of the whole picture! But when the time of perfection comes, these partial things will become useless.

When I was a child, I spoke and thought and reasoned as a child. But when I grew up, I put away childish things. Now we see things imperfectly, like puzzling reflections in a mirror, but then we will see everything with perfect clarity. All that I know now is partial and incomplete, but then I will know everything completely, just as God now knows me completely.

Three things will last forever—faith, hope, and love—and the greatest of these is love. (1 Corinthians 13 NLT)

If you got through that and didn't feel at all inadequate, I salute you! Let's start at the top. In verses 1–3, we are told that we can do everything right—we can be "good people"—but if we don't love others, we have nothing. If that's not eye-opening, I don't know what is. That's why love is so important. If you have faith that can move mountains, that's incredible, but if you don't love others, it's irrelevant. Wow. I hope you're getting the severity of this. It's not just nice to love others, it's crucial.

Truthfully, this is the part that always convicts me:

> Love is patient and kind. Love is not jealous or boastful or proud or rude. It does not demand its own way. It is not irritable, and it keeps no record of being wronged. It does not rejoice about injustice but rejoices whenever the truth wins out. Love never gives up, never loses faith, is always hopeful, and endures through every circumstance. (1 Corinthians 13:4–7 NLT)

I cannot in good conscience say that these verses describe me or how I show love. I truly wish they did, but I don't know if, as humans, we will ever get to a point where we can truthfully say this about ourselves. However, it gives us something to strive toward. It gives us a picture of who God is and who He has called us to be.

So here is your challenge. Take one piece of this scripture, whichever verse (or verses) stands out to you most, and write it on a Post-it Note. Now stick it to your mirror, your fridge, or even your coffee maker, wherever you know you'll see it in the morning. Read it every morning for a week straight and try to live it throughout those seven days. Then pick a different verse and do that one for another week. Keep going until you get through the whole thing. You can also break up the verses. For example, you could write, "Love is not irritable," and work on not letting the little things get to you. Don't get irritated by the people around you, and really work on that one thought for a full week. Even make it your phone lock screen if you need to!

Love, in theory, should be easy, right? But I think it's safe to say that through our own experiences and through reading scripture, it's really not. Feelings of love can come and go like the wind, but real, genuine love is a choice, and it takes effort. Are you willing to put in the work to really love others the way God calls us to?

Reflection/Discussion Questions

- Have you ever had a bad neighbor?
- Have you ever been a bad neighbor?
- Do you think the people in your life know you by your love?
- How does this scripture make you feel? "If I had the gift of prophecy, and if I understood all of God's secret plans and possessed all knowledge, and if I had such faith that I could move mountains, but didn't love others, I would be nothing" (1 Corinthians 13:2 NLT).
- Which verse will you use to start the challenge at the end of the chapter?
- After reading through chapter 10, are you willing to put in the work to really love others the way God calls us to?

Chapter 11
FAMILY TIES

The giving of love is an education in itself.
—Eleanor Roosevelt

One thing I really want to emphasize is that *love is a choice*. Galatians 6:5 in the New Living Translation Bible says, "For we are each responsible for our own conduct." We are responsible for the choices we make—the good, the bad, and the ugly ones too.

We make choices every day. From the moment we wake up in the morning until the moment we go to sleep at night. We make those choices based on different things—convenience, emotions (what we feel at that moment), previous experiences, peer pressure, pressure from families, our insecurities, our fears … That's how we make most of our choices, but is that biblical? Is that how we should be making our choices?

We may not realize how small choices can impact our lives in a big way, but they can—especially when it comes to choosing to love people. You know, there is a point along the Continental Divide, high in the Rocky Mountains in Colorado, where the waters of a small stream separate. Big deal, right? It wouldn't seem to matter much whether a drop of water goes to the left or to the right. But the outcome for those drops of water is totally different. One drop goes to the west and eventually flows into the Colorado River and empties into the Gulf of California and the Pacific Ocean. Another drop goes east until it flows into the Mississippi River and dumps into the Gulf of Mexico and the Atlantic Ocean. Two drops of water, two entirely different destinations, but one small turning point that determines the outcome.

Many choices in life are like that. At the time they may not seem significant or life-changing, but those choices set in motion a series of events that shape your life and the lives of your children and grandchildren after you. If you choose to hold on to anger and resentment instead of embracing forgiveness and grace, your heart hardens and you carry bitterness into everything you do. It can affect your family, your work, and you'd better believe that it will significantly affect your relationship with God. The Bible says that we are responsible for our own conduct (Galatians 6:5 NLT); God gave us free will and we're responsible for what we do with it. Choosing love isn't always the easiest choice—in fact, it's almost never the easy route—but it can set the trajectory of your day, your week, your month, your year, even your entire future on a different path.

Now with all that said, I have a confession to make. I don't have this love stuff all figured out. I am still learning to choose love. Sometimes that choice is an easy one, like when it comes to my kids who are driving me bonkers, but they are so perfect at the same time and it's easier in those moments to choose love and grace instead of getting angry and yelling at them or saying, "I told you so." I also have people in my life who are wonderful and just want to help me and want to be a part of my life, but on some days I find it hard to show them love. And then there are people who I have to choose every day to love, often making a conscious effort to choose love over my pride and my hurt. Love isn't easy, and it's a lifelong journey.

I can say that yes, as a general blanket statement, I love people, but I've come to realize that my actions haven't always said the same thing. I can say I love my family or I love people, but do the things I do and say show the world that I truly mean those words? I hate to get all cliché on you, but it's true what they say: actions really do speak louder than words. Look at this woman who, if she did say anything to Jesus, it isn't recorded in the Bible, but her actions are recorded for generation after generation to read about and learn from.

> One of the Pharisees invited Jesus to have dinner with him. So he went to the Pharisee's house. He took his place at the table. There was a woman in that town who had lived a sinful life. She learned that Jesus was eating at the Pharisee's house. So she came there with a special jar of perfume. She stood behind Jesus and cried at his feet. And she began to wet his feet with her tears. Then she wiped them with her hair. She kissed them and poured perfume on them.
>
> The Pharisee who had invited Jesus saw this. He said to himself, "If this man were a prophet, he would know who is touching him. He would know what kind of woman she is. She is a sinner!"
>
> Jesus answered him, "Simon, I have something to tell you."
>
> "Tell me, teacher," he said.

"Two people owed money to a certain lender. One owed him 500 silver coins. The other owed him 50 silver coins. Neither of them had the money to pay him back. So he let them go without paying. Which of them will love him more?"

> Simon replied, "I suppose the one who owed the most money."
>
> "You are right," Jesus said.

Then he turned toward the woman. He said to Simon, "Do you see this woman? I came into your house. You did not give me any water to wash my feet. But she wet my feet with her tears and wiped them with her hair. You did not give me a kiss. But this woman has not stopped kissing my feet since I came in. You did not put any olive oil on my head. But she has poured this perfume on my feet. So I tell you this. Her many sins have been forgiven. She has shown that she understands this ***by her great acts of love***. But whoever has been forgiven only a little loves only a little."

Then Jesus said to her, "Your sins are forgiven."

The other guests began to talk about this among themselves. They said, "Who is this who even forgives sins?"

Jesus said to the woman, "Your faith has saved you. Go in peace." (Luke 7:36–50 NIV, emphasis mine)

Think about it this way: If a guy says he loves his girlfriend and then abuses her, hits her, screams at her, and berates her, what should we pay more attention to: his words or his actions? Which shows his true colors? Friends, let's be honest. It's easy to lie. Some people are even really good at it and even make a living from it. It can be easy to change your words based on what you think someone wants or needs to hear in that moment or what you want to portray about yourself to others. But our actions speak to our true character—especially how we act when we think no one is watching. Did you show love and compassion to the beggar on the street corner or jump to the other side of the road to avoid him? Jesus told the story of the good Samaritan for a reason, friends. Do you return the cash you saw fall

Hard to Love

out of that lady's purse or take it and even go so far as to call it a "blessing" or an "answered prayer"? I promise you, in this situation, the only blessing you'll get is in heaven and it'll be for returning it.

All of that to tell you that I have been on a journey of learning to show my love to my mother-in-law with my actions. I'll preface this by saying that I truly do love my mother-in-law, she is so wonderful, and she always has the very best intentions for me and my family. I genuinely love the relationship and authentic friendship we have today and I am so thankful to have her in my life. She is a blessing I never expected but I am so thankful for.

That said, shortly after my husband and I were officially married, I started to experience some challenges in my relationship with her (completely unknown to her because they were all my own issues). Like I said, she's wonderful and I cherish our relationship today. But once my husband and I got married, out of nowhere (at least it felt that way), I got very territorial over my husband and our new life together and really felt the need to establish myself as the woman of my household—the *only* woman of my household. To be honest, I believe this is a pretty common struggle between women and their mothers-in-law and it's an issue that should be dealt with ASAP before damage is done to a marriage or family relationships.

I can tell you that when I realized this was happening, I handled it the wrong way. And by that, I mean that I didn't handle it at all. I thought I was being loving by bottling everything up and pretending like I didn't have this inner conflict but that wasn't loving at all. That was my first mistake. My second mistake (maybe it should actually be tied for first) was that I rarely talked to my husband about it. Which, in retrospect, is so ridiculous because I literally tell him everything—even when he might wish I didn't! Anyway, once we had kids, I felt extra pressure and got really tired, really quickly, of all the unsolicited advice and the unannounced visits. My mother-in-law has always had good intentions. I know that, especially looking back when I'm not sleep-deprived and struggling to survive the newborn phase. But it didn't always feel that way. Lack of sleep coupled with postpartum hormones doesn't always paint the clearest picture. Knowing and feeling are very different things.

When I considered talking to her about how I was feeling, I always told myself it was better not to because she had her own insecurities, as we all do, and approaching or confronting any issues I was having with her would be very difficult (at least that's what I convinced myself of). I will also note that one of the main reasons for this was because I saw glimpses of my past self—my past insecurities—in her and that can be hard for me. I always thought that would be something that filled me with compassion and understanding because of my past, but surprisingly it was triggering for me instead and has been something I've worked on since that realization.

I also didn't want her to take out any tension I had with her on my husband. I desperately wanted to protect him from that potential conflict and guilt. So I walked on eggshells and avoided my concerns and issues, no matter what they were, which just led to them piling up into a big ol' brick wall. Each encounter would lay another brick and I would get more frustrated. So looking back now, I can confidently say that I did everything wrong. Literally everything. There were even times during it all that I knew I wasn't doing what I should, but I wanted to avoid the conflict, the hurt—all of it—so I did. But eventually I got fed up. It was causing tension between me and my husband (marriage tip: brick walls aren't helpful in your relationship) so I'd come to the end of my rope.

It took a lot of self-reflection and some real work to realize that the real issue wasn't my mother-in-law at all; it was my pride. I wanted to be right. I didn't want to lay down my pride and hear (not even follow, just hear) her advice or opinions because I knew what was best for my family and that was that. The truth is I honestly do believe that I know what is best for my family because I know my family best. There's nothing wrong with that. But that doesn't mean that I can't show grace. That doesn't mean that I can't have conversations. That doesn't mean that I can't allow other people in my life to feel heard and accepted. What harm could that possibly do? Other than maybe a little hit to my ego, absolutely none. No damage whatsoever.

On the other hand, the way I handled it before was causing damage to my relationship with my mother-in-law, my relationship with my husband, my own personal peace and, in turn, my relationship with God. Why would I want to stay in that place? So I learned that in order to love others effectively, not just say, "Of course I love my mother-in-law," with an exaggerated sigh, I needed to lay down my pride and show humility. It was difficult at first, which really just goes to show what a problem pride had become for me, but now I know that holding onto resentment and frustration and having imaginary arguments in my head is way more exhausting than showing love and grace. That doesn't mean I always have to agree, take the advice, or avoid confrontation when it's needed. It just means that I can now approach all of these things from a place of genuine love, without any intent to hurt the other person or prove/validate myself or my worth. It's freeing. Maintaining an open and honest dialogue in any relationship is like a breath of fresh air and it is so important—that includes our relationship with God. I also learned along the way that allowing someone else to voice their two cents can really make them feel heard and that, in turn, can make them feel loved. And if I can show love to the people in my life simply by listening to them, that's something I am definitely going to do.

Loving people means giving up the desire to be right and giving in to the desire to be like Jesus.

> By this all will know that you are My disciples, if
> you have love for one another. (John 13:35 (NKJV)

It's taken time and I have to constantly check my heart, as we all should be doing on a regular basis, but God has shown me grace and my relationship with my mother-in-law is incredibly different now. I'll give you an example.

If you are lucky enough to not be familiar with or have had any experiences with dementia, please count yourself extremely blessed. It's a really difficult condition not just for the person diagnosed but for everyone in that person's life as well. Unfortunately, I have had some experience with dementia, particularly a form that involved a lot of paranoia. That said, I'm going to try to keep this long story somewhat short.

One day, I was completely taken off guard when someone I was once very close with would no longer take my calls, see me, or have anything to do with me. I came to understand soon thereafter that it was because of the aforementioned paranoia. The dementia had created a malicious narrative in their mind and memories about me and there was nothing I could do about it. I couldn't defend myself; I couldn't present the truth because in this situation, the truth didn't hold any weight. And this was someone whom I loved dearly and desperately wanted to continue a relationship with, but the dementia had made it impossible. I was understandably devastated when I found out that they had cut me out of their life, especially because there was nothing I could do about it. I was completely powerless in the situation because their brain literally could not reason anymore and all I wanted to do was cry. Actually, that's not true, all I wanted to cry *and* I wanted to call my mother-in-law. I don't know why exactly, but at that moment, I just really wanted to talk to her and cry with her. She's the one I wanted to share this with and she's the one person I wanted to mourn the loss of that relationship with. That's love.

Another example is when my mother-in-law lost her father. I felt such a deep compassion and empathy for her during that time that I knew my heart had changed from what it used to be; the walls were all broken down and my heart literally ached as I saw her in pain. I just wanted her to know how loved she was, and I wanted to help ease any part of her pain that I could.

Hard to Love

Loving others isn't always easy, but it's always worth it. Not because of what we get in return. We won't always get love back; we won't always get a fuzzy feeling inside. Quite the opposite actually. Sometimes we can feel cheated or taken advantage of. Sometimes we feel like we wasted our time. Other times we can change a person's life with some love and kindness. Either way, God has called us to love; therefore, every single time we go out of our way to show love, it is worth it. Because the world will know we are His disciples by our love. I don't know about you, but I want that to be true about my life.

If we really look at that concept—they will know us by our love—can you imagine if someone didn't come to know Jesus, they missed out on salvation, because of your unwillingness to love? That's a very sobering thought. Don't get me wrong. We are not responsible for salvation; the Holy Spirit works in people's hearts and He will do what He will do, no matter what. But if we fail to show love, we aren't giving Him the opportunity to do what He can do. See how that works? Even if our love and kindness can remove one brick from someone else's wall, that creates more space for God's light to get through.

Another way to look at it is through the lens of the church. Why do we have the church? Why did Jesus die for the church? God wants our participation. He wants to love the world through us—the church. He wants people to see Him through us. That is how we change hearts. That is how we change the world.

How different would our world look today if our leaders led with love instead of pursuing political will, power, and pride? I honestly can't even imagine a world like that.

The moral of this story is that Jesus gave love freely to us and we need to give it freely to others. It takes work. Are you ready to do that? Are you ready to live a life led by love?

Reflection/Discussion Questions

- What do you think of Eleanor Roosevelt's quote at the beginning of the chapter ("The giving of love is an education in itself.")?
- Why is love a choice?
- Have you ever made a small choice that had a big impact?
- Read Luke 7:36–50 (NIV) again and ask God to speak to you about it. What is He saying?
- Do you have any family members (or friends, coworkers, etc.) that you need to do a better job of showing love to?
- Are there any relationships where you need to give up the desire to be right and give in to the desire to be like Jesus?
- Are you ready to live a life led by love?

Chapter 12

THE SAMARITANS

Have you ever passed someone on the street and took a few extra steps to the side in an effort to avoid being within a five-foot radius of them? It sounds silly when I write it out, but I've done it. I have seen someone who looks very different from me, someone "scary" or angry, even sick or desperate looking—the outcasts, so to speak—and I have kept my eyes down and tried to avoid them. I'm not proud of it, but that's the honest truth. That's not very loving of me, is it? And if we look to our ultimate example Jesus, He didn't do that. Not once.

In fact, the best example of this is in the New Testament when we read about the Samaritans. Yes, we will discuss the story of the Good Samaritan, but I actually want to start off with the story of the Samaritan woman at the well. Let's read John 4:1–30 (NLT) and then we'll get into why this story is so significant when it comes to loving others.

Jesus and the Samaritan Woman

> Jesus knew the Pharisees had heard that he was baptizing and making more disciples than John (though Jesus himself didn't baptize them—his disciples did). So he left Judea and returned to Galilee.
>
> He had to go through Samaria on the way. Eventually he came to the Samaritan village of Sychar, near

the field that Jacob gave to his son Joseph. Jacob's well was there; and Jesus, tired from the long walk, sat wearily beside the well about noontime. Soon a Samaritan woman came to draw water, and Jesus said to her, "Please give me a drink." He was alone at the time because his disciples had gone into the village to buy some food.

The woman was surprised, for Jews refuse to have anything to do with Samaritans. She said to Jesus, "You are a Jew, and I am a Samaritan woman. Why are you asking me for a drink?"

Jesus replied, "If you only knew the gift God has for you and who you are speaking to, you would ask me, and I would give you living water."

"But sir, you don't have a rope or a bucket," she said, "and this well is very deep. Where would you get this living water? And besides, do you think you're greater than our ancestor Jacob, who gave us this well? How can you offer better water than he and his sons and his animals enjoyed?"

Jesus replied, "Anyone who drinks this water will soon become thirsty again. But those who drink the water I give will never be thirsty again. It becomes a fresh, bubbling spring within them, giving them eternal life."

"Please, sir," the woman said, "give me this water! Then I'll never be thirsty again, and I won't have to come here to get water."

"Go and get your husband," Jesus told her.

"I don't have a husband," the woman replied.

Jesus said, "You're right! You don't have a husband—for you have had five husbands, and you aren't even married to the man you're living with now. You certainly spoke the truth!"

"Sir," the woman said, "you must be a prophet. So tell me, why is it that you Jews insist that Jerusalem is the only place of worship, while we Samaritans claim it is here at Mount Gerizim, where our ancestors worshiped?"

Jesus replied, "Believe me, dear woman, the time is coming when it will no longer matter whether you worship the Father on this mountain or in Jerusalem. You Samaritans know very little about the one you worship, while we Jews know all about him, for salvation comes through the Jews. But the time is coming—indeed it's here now—when true worshipers will worship the Father in spirit and in truth. The Father is looking for those who will worship him that way. For God is Spirit, so those who worship him must worship in spirit and in truth."

The woman said, "I know the Messiah is coming—the one who is called Christ. When he comes, he will explain everything to us."

Then Jesus told her, "I am the Messiah!"

Just then his disciples came back. They were shocked to find him talking to a woman, but none of them had the nerve to ask, "What do you want with her?" or "Why are you talking to her?" The woman left her water jar beside the well and ran back to the village, telling everyone, "Come and see a man who told me everything I ever did! Could he possibly be the Messiah?" So the people came streaming from the village to see him.

Wow. There is so much to talk about in this particular piece of scripture. First, as we know, Jews and Samaritans were not considered friendly back then. In fact, they were much closer to enemies. The Samaritan woman even mentions this to Jesus. "Umm, why are you talking to me? Do you even know who I am?" Of course He knew. He knew who she was and He knew she'd be there that day. His response was along the lines of "I do know who you are and now you get to know who I AM."

Words cannot describe how much I love this story! First things first, it's important to note that this woman was an outcast. How do we know that? She was drawing water from the well at noon, the hottest time of the day. Why is that important? Because most women came early in the morning when it was much cooler. The mornings at the well also served as their social time; it was the nail salon or the Starbucks of that day. But this woman went to the well when she knew no one else would be there so that no one would be around to see and ostracize her. She was not only despised by the Jewish people for simply being a Samaritan, but she was also outcast by her own people for the life she lived and the things she'd done. She had had five husbands and was now living in sin with a man she wasn't married to. Those were not acceptable circumstances back then and, to avoid the shame, she avoided people and therefore their judgment. Can you blame her?

Knowing all of this, Jesus chose this woman—a Samaritan

woman—to tell, "I am the Messiah!" This is the first time that Jesus states outright that He is the Messiah. And He chose to reveal this truth to a rejected Samaritan woman who was living in sin. *How incredible is that?* But we shouldn't be surprised by this choice. After all, Jesus also said,

> When Jesus heard this, he told them, "Healthy people don't need a doctor—sick people do. I have come to call not those who think they are righteous, but those who know they are sinners." (Mark 2:17 NLT)

This moment with the Samaritan woman is so significant for so many reasons. Not only did Jesus reveal Himself as the Messiah to a Samaritan (mind blown!), but to a woman who would have been seen as less than in the eyes of that society. Keep in mind that it was very rare for a Jewish priest to engage in open conversation with any woman at that time. But Jesus was different. Jesus *is* different. *Jesus saw past her sin and saw her as a person.* Now don't get me wrong. He saw her sin and called her out on it, but He also saw her as a person—a child of God—whom He came to save. *His love was bigger than her sin.*

Another interesting detail to mention is that Jesus could have gone around Samaria on his trip, like most Jewish people did back then. (Seriously, the Jews avoided Samaria and Samaritans like the plague.) But the Bible says He *had* to go through Samaria. After reading the scriptures, we can see that he had to go through Samaria because He had a divine appointment to keep. He could have taken a different route. He could have gone to another well. He could have let the Samaritan woman draw the water and leave in silence while He waited for someone less sinful to come along. He could have done it differently, but Jesus was so intentional about everything He did and everything He said. He loved the outcasts and He still does. We are called to do the same.

Let's also appreciate the fact that it wasn't just *her* life that was changed through this encounter with Jesus's love and kindness either. No, she shares her experience with her entire village! One encounter with Jesus and her shame was gone. All these people that she had been avoiding, that she was hiding from, embarrassed to be seen by, she ran right up to them and told them what had happened! Jesus showing love and kindness to this woman changed her life and the lives of many others. That's what Jesus's love does; it's contagious and it's beautiful. It changes you.

Another example of this is from arguably one of the best-known parables in the Bible. That's right, we're back to the parable of the Good Samaritan.

The Parable of the Good Samaritan

> On one occasion an expert in the law stood up to test Jesus. "Teacher," he asked, "what must I do to inherit eternal life?"
>
> "What is written in the Law?" he replied. "How do you read it?"
>
> He answered, "'Love the Lord your God with all your heart and with all your soul and with all your strength and with all your mind'; and, 'Love your neighbor as yourself.'"
>
> "You have answered correctly," Jesus replied. "Do this and you will live."
>
> But he wanted to justify himself, so he asked Jesus, "And who is my neighbor?"

In reply Jesus said: "A man was going down from Jerusalem to Jericho, when he was attacked by robbers. They stripped him of his clothes, beat him and went away, leaving him half dead. A priest happened to be going down the same road, and when he saw the man, he passed by on the other side. So too, a Levite, when he came to the place and saw him, passed by on the other side. But a Samaritan, as he traveled, came where the man was; and when he saw him, he took pity on him. He went to him and bandaged his wounds, pouring on oil and wine. Then he put the man on his own donkey, brought him to an inn and took care of him. The next day he took out two denarii and gave them to the innkeeper. 'Look after him,' he said, 'and when I return, I will reimburse you for any extra expense you may have.'

"Which of these three do you think was a neighbor to the man who fell into the hands of robbers?"

The expert in the law replied, "The one who had mercy on him."

Jesus told him, "Go and do likewise." (Luke 10:25–37 NIV)

    I have to admit that while I'm glad this story is well-known, I think the popularity has made it less powerful than it actually is. We see it as a nice story that tells us to be kind to people but it is so much more than that. This story is so impactful because not only does Jesus use it to instruct us on how to treat others (we'll get into that in a minute), but He also makes a point to mention that religious people, such as the priest, were not treating others that way. *Calling ourselves "Christians" does not automatically make us Christlike.* The priest avoided someone who needed help. How ironic is that? It was the Samaritan, an "enemy" of the Jewish people, who stopped and offered compassion, assistance, and ended up saving this man's life. If that is how we are supposed to treat people, we have some work to do, wouldn't you agree?

How often do you stop to give change to someone begging on the street? How often do you offer to buy them lunch or give them your jacket if they're cold? How often are you willing to be inconvenienced, either by time or money, to help someone you don't know and who may never be able to repay you, or even say thank-you? I think the answer for most of us is not often enough.

This Samaritan man was going somewhere but he stopped when he saw someone in need, thus disrupting his schedule. And he didn't just stop to check on him; he tended to this man. Then he gave up his luxury and his convenience by putting the injured man on his donkey and walking him to an inn. Then the Samaritan man spent his own money to ensure the injured man was taken care of in his absence. I'd say that coming across this injured man on the street was extremely inconvenient and even uncomfortable, but we don't hear the Samaritan complaining about it. We only see him caring for someone in need, no questions asked. It was someone he didn't know, but he was willing to be uncomfortable and inconvenienced to help him. Are you? Am I? It's a powerful story on its own but even more so when you start asking these questions.

Jesus told this parable after being asked "and who is my neighbor?" so we can safely assume that when Jesus tells us to love our neighbors, that we can consider all people our neighbors, not just those who live close to us or that we do life with on a regular basis.

As followers of Jesus, we need to follow His example. Jesus made it very clear through these two stories that we are to love people, even people who society shuns, even people who are smack dab in the middle of sin, even people that others avoid and pretend not to see, even those who other people are judging. We are called to love those people. That's a tall order, but I challenge you to think about how you can start doing that today.

Throughout scripture, we learn that Jesus sought out the outcasts of His day, including the tax collectors. In order to completely grasp the weight of this, you need to understand that tax collectors were held in the lowest esteem, similar to prostitutes. They were the bottom feeders that no one liked and everyone avoided. Basically all the people who were considered by society as unsavory and "less than." Who are the tax collectors in your world? The person you avoid eye contact with when you walk by them on the street? Is it the person who looks and thinks completely opposite of you? How about the person posting racist slurs and bigotry on social media? Or maybe it's the person who lives in a way that you don't agree with? Could it be the murderer on death row? Or the person you gossip about to your best friend, "I can't believe he/she did that"? Let's face the facts here: These are people. These are people created in God's image—whether they know that or not and whether that's the first thing we see when we look at them or not. The reality is that we are called to love them. We are called to show them love the way Jesus showed love. That doesn't mean we condone or support their sin, just that we lead with love.

One of the values of my home church is "Love is our answer." I love that. Love needs to be our answer because it was Jesus's answer.

Stick with me for one more note about the Samaritans before closing this chapter out.

Opposition from Samaritans

> As the time drew near for him to ascend to heaven, Jesus resolutely set out for Jerusalem. He sent messengers ahead to a Samaritan village to prepare for his arrival. But the people of the village did not welcome Jesus because he was on his way to Jerusalem. When James and John saw this, they said to Jesus,

"Lord, should we call down fire from heaven to burn them up?" But Jesus turned and rebuked them. So they went on to another village. (Luke 9:51–56 NLT)

Now at first glance this may not seem relevant to our talk about loving others, but these few verses are enormously significant. James and John are angry with the Samaritans for not welcoming Jesus with open arms and they ask if they can call down fire from heaven to teach them a lesson, like Elijah did in the Old Testament. At this suggestion, Jesus rebukes them. To rebuke means to sternly disapprove of or to reprimand so obviously Jesus was not happy with them. His response teaches us that the old eye-for-eye sentiment is dead and gone. His response shows that it is better not to retaliate or seek revenge. That is the new standard, that is the New Testament of the Bible, and that is how we need to act. We'll get more into this soon when we talk about loving our enemies. *(Who's excited for that one?)* But it was worth mentioning here as well and it gives you something to look forward to, I hope.

Reflection/Discussion Questions

- Have you ever avoided someone on the street because they looked different or "scary"?
- Why do you think Jesus chose a sinful Samaritan woman to reveal Himself as the Messiah to?
- Have you ever felt like something in your life was a "divine appointment"?
- How can you show love to the outcasts you encounter?
- Have you ever encountered someone who calls themselves "Christian" but their actions and attitudes aren't very Christlike?
- How often are you willing to be inconvenienced for the sake of someone else—someone you don't know?

Chapter 13
HABITS

If you've been paying attention, you're already well aware that we need to lay down pride in order to love the way we are called to love. Laying down your pride sounds easy, right? One simple step and you're good to go. Let's get loving! I hate to break it to you, but it is the exact opposite of that and it will probably make you want to kick and scream for the first little while. It's hard. Loving people is hard! It requires work. And not just a little bit of work. I'm talking Rihanna work. (You know the song ... "Work, work, work, work, work, work.")

One of the biggest areas we all need to look at and put in the work to get us on the right track is our habits. We all develop habits—many of which are unconscious. We need to figure out which of our habits are harming us and others and we need to change them. One great way to discover any annoying, weird, or unhealthy habits is to have children. You heard me. Our children become our mirrors. They reflect our behaviors—good and bad—because they watch us constantly. Literally, I am never alone. Because that's how they learn.

I didn't know I had a terrible habit of picking at my fingernails until my daughter, when she was three years old, developed the same habit and she *could not stop.* Her nails could be ripped down to the skin, sometimes bleeding, and no matter what we tried, she kept doing it. Where did she learn such a gross, bizarre habit to begin with? Watching me. I'm her caretaker, her best friend, and she spends every waking hour by my side. She notices the things I do that I don't even know I'm doing. And no, I don't rip my nails down to the skin until they bleed because I'm an adult and I have self-control. I just play with them and sometimes pick at them in a fidgety way because, well, I don't know why. I just do. But a three-year-old doesn't have the intellectual maturity to understand boundaries yet. She couldn't understand fidgeting. She didn't know how to stop something that she doesn't even realize she's doing most of the time. Habits. We all have them.

Switching gears for a minute, I want you to do me a favor and take a moment, a self-reflection if you will, and think about how you tend to deal with difficult people. Do you give them attitude or do you give them the benefit of the doubt? Do you roll your eyes when you see them or give them a genuine smile? Do you gossip about them behind their backs or pray for them and bless them? Or are you not sure how to answer these questions because you either pretend they don't exist or don't want to give them a second thought?

Now think about how you typically react when someone does or says something that makes you mad. Seriously, think about it. I won't make you post your response to social media so it doesn't matter whether it's a "good" response or not. We're all growing and learning here.

Do you lash out? Scream at them? Do you stonewall (shut down completely)? Do you run and hide? Do you ghost them? Do you call your significant other or your best friend to tell them all the horrible things about that person? Do you obsessively replay the confrontation in your head thinking about what you should have said (if anything) or how you should have handled it differently?

Not many people would answer the above reflections with "I respond with patience, love, and grace, asking how I can help the person in question." If you did answer that way, put your bookmark in here and go eat some celebratory ice cream because you are ahead of the curve.

The truth is most of us have a tendency to react from a place of emotion in these situations, rather than respond from a place of grace. Unfortunately for us, our reactions build habits over time.

For example, one habit that was hard for me to break was making passive-aggressive comments or "digs" when I felt slighted. This unhealthy habit was a result of a lifetime of very low self-esteem and therefore always feeling the need to have the last word to prove my point, to give myself value. I always needed to defend myself somehow. I also used to bring other people down because I thought so low of myself that I tried to bring others down with me in an attempt to make myself feel a little less than nothing. Honestly, that's still hard to admit, never mind write and share with the world. I've come a long way, but it's been a lot of work. And it still is! I still have bad habits and tendencies that creep up and I need to be self-aware and check my heart regularly in order to keep myself healthy. It also helps to have a partner who is willing to call me out and walk with me through whatever I'm facing (shout out to my amazing husband!).

Back to these passive-aggressive digs that used to wreak havoc in my life. I used to do this with my husband a lot. More often than not, he had no idea that something was even bothering me at the time I'd make these comments so it really threw him off—and by threw him off, I mean either confused him or, after a few too many, ticked him off. It caused tension between us because, well, we're human and how could it not? I tried to stop but it had become such a habit in my life to get that last word or defend myself when I got offended (which used to be a lot more often than I care to admit) that I really struggled to stop. A lifetime of defending myself, defending my worth, and trying to prove myself wasn't something I was able to just quit overnight. It took a lot of work and personal growth. It took relying on the Holy Spirit to help me realize what I was doing in those moments and to hold my tongue, pray, and move forward.

Here's an example of what these passive-aggressive comments looked like. My husband would comment after a day of work that he had a headache and needed to lie down. I would say, "OK," but having had a really tough day at home with two toddlers, I would then say under my breath, "Must be nice to be able to take a break and relax in some peace and quiet," or something along those lines. Now that you're judging me on my extreme pettiness and horrible bad habits, I get it. It sounds terrible, but guess what. We all have habits and tendencies that need some work so let's look at yours.

Take a couple of minutes to think and/or pray about any tendencies or habits you might have that need to be dealt with. Anything that could be hindering you from loving the way God wants you to love. Write it out so it can stare at you from the page, even if only for a few minutes. Then feel free to rip it up, shred it, set it on fire—whatever floats your boat.

Seriously, put this book down and don't come back until you do this. And don't rush it. This is an incredibly important step in the process. Here's a prayer to help you get started:

> Father God,
>
> Thank You for loving me in ways beyond comprehension. I want to love people in the way that You have called me to love them. My heart is open. Please show me any areas in my life, any hurts or bad habits, that are hindering my ability to love.
>
> In Jesus's name, amen.

Now that you've looked at yourself and hopefully identified habits or tendencies that need some work, let's look at what God wants from us.

When I was trying to break the bad habit mentioned above, I read this scripture in Ephesians (emphasis mine):

> "Do not let any unwholesome talk come out of your mouths, but only what is helpful for **building others up** according to their needs, that it may benefit those who listen." (Ephesians 4:29 NIV)

Hard to Love

Gulp. It doesn't take a rocket scientist to know that scripture definitely did not describe me or my passive-aggressive comment habit. So I was left asking, "Now what?" I knew I had my work cut out for me. I would need to work on laying down my pride, showing humility, and extending grace. Easy peasy, right? Ha! I wish. The thing with showing grace is that you can't tell people you're showing them grace or you aren't actually showing them grace. So when someone cuts you off in traffic, you can't follow them until they stop, roll down your window, and say, "I was going to flip you off but I'm showing grace today," and continue on your way. If my husband sits down to enjoy a nice cup of hot coffee in the morning before the kids get up while I unload the dishwasher from the night before, make snacks and lunches for school, pack backpacks, and tidy up the kitchen counter, I can't tell him I'm *letting* him enjoy that coffee while I rush around doing everything just so I can drink lukewarm coffee I've already microwaved twice. You don't get external credit for showing grace; it doesn't work that way.

Another thing to note is that often the source of our acting out is our own unmet expectations. In this last example, my husband didn't know I wanted help in the mornings because I didn't ask for help. I wanted him to just know I wanted help and to just do it without me having to ask. That doesn't seem fair, does it? And when I do ask for help, he is happy to do it, but I needed to get to a place where I could let go of my pride and be both direct and vulnerable enough to ask for help. I also worked to change my mindset to one of gratitude. Hectic mornings are a byproduct of the incredible family that I spent years praying for. When I look at it that way, it changes things.

Let's look at grace. It's a word that Christians use all the time—especially as middle names for our children. But do we really understand grace?

The word *grace* means mercy, pardon, a special favor, privilege, disposition to or an act or instance of kindness, courtesy, or clemency.

Grace is undeserved acceptance and love received from another.[5] In the New Testament, the Greek word for *grace* is *charis*. It's used approximately 150 times in the New Testament, depending on the translation. In the Greek language, *charis* originally referred to a delightful quality in a person, an attribute that brought contentment to others. Eventually its meaning morphed and was later used how we see it in the New Testament to describe the concept of freely doing a favor without any expectation of something in return.[6] In other words, grace doesn't keep tabs.

One of the worst habits I developed over the years was having pretend arguments in my head. Do you ever do that? It sounds ridiculous when I write it out on this page, but that's what I used to do, and if I'm honest, I still catch myself doing it from time to time. If I pick my kids from the babysitter's house and the oldest tells me in the car that they watched a bunch of TV and ate sausages, cheese, and cookies for lunch, it makes my left eye twitch. I'm not a helicopter mom, but I did (and still do) limit screen time, especially when my kiddos were only two and three, and I try to feed them healthy things. Yes, they get treats. I'm not super strict, but on occasion, I have specifically asked for certain things to not be given to them because they are so insanely unhealthy for them. So what do I do? I argue in my head. It's embarrassing to admit, but that's what I do. I debate whether to say something now, say something later, or just simply let it go and don't say anything at all. And then I play out all possible scenarios in my head. I think about what I should have said and what they would have said back ... Ugh. Why am I like this? I don't know, but I can tell you that this is one of the hardest habits to break. The amount of time and energy that goes into completely made-up arguments is atrocious. Seriously, I hope no one ever does that math. Why do we allow others to live rent free

---

[5] *Bible Dictionary*, 678.
[6] *Bible Dictionary*, 679.

in our heads like this? I don't have the answer to that, but I know it has to stop.

Especially because the Bible says,

> For God has not given us a spirit of fear, but of power and of love and of a **sound mind**. (2 Timothy 1:7 NKJV, emphasis mine)

A lot of loving people and breaking habits actually starts in our minds. Once we realize that, we've taken a huge step forward. I say that because we can't always control our emotions, but with God, we can control our minds so that means we can do it. God has given us the power to do it.

I understand that all of this is much simpler in theory than in practice, but let's start simple. Choose a person who you find somewhat hard to love. It could be someone you've had previous conflict with or someone who doesn't even know they get on your nerves. Choose to do something nice for that person today. Compliment them, bring them a coffee, tell them you appreciate something they do, etc. Just one simple act of love, in spite of your feelings, is the first step.

Reflection/Discussion Questions

- Do you have any strange or less-than-desirable habits?
- How do you tend to deal with difficult people?
- How do you typically react when someone does or says something that makes you mad? Do you get defensive? Stonewall? Run away?
- What tendencies or habits do you have that could be hindering you from loving others the way God has called you to?
- Do you get offended easily?
- Do you ever have pretend arguments in your head?

Part 4
LOVE YOUR ENEMIES

Chapter 14
EYE FOR AN EYE

Well, here we are, the part of the book about loving your enemies. This subject matter might not scare you, and if that is the case, I salute you! To the rest of us, it'll be OK. I promise. Loving our enemies is hard but worth it. With God in your corner, you've got this.

The verse below didn't always bring joy to my heart, but I can honestly say now that it is one of my favorite verses because it really shows the character of Jesus and how drastically things have changed under the new covenant.

> "You have heard that it was said, 'Love your neighbor and hate your enemy.' But I tell you, love your enemies and pray for those who persecute you, that you may be children of your Father in heaven. He causes his sun to rise on the evil and the good, and sends rain on the righteous and the unrighteous. If you love those who love you, what reward will you get? Are not even the tax collectors doing that?" (Matthew 5:43–46 NIV)

Loving your neighbors will eventually get easier and even become a habit in your day-to-day life. Loving your enemies, on the other hand, is one of the hardest things we are called to do. Trust me. I speak from experience.

What messages did we receive about this growing up? Personally,

I remember a lot of movies about revenge and getting even—not necessarily as a central plot but somewhere within the story. It was just a normal, acceptable concept. I also remember the saying "An eye for an eye" very clearly. Where did I first hear it? I have no idea, but I remember knowing it from a young age. It was just part of the regular, accepted vernacular so I never questioned where it came from. As it turns out, it's an ancient Babylonian, biblical, Roman principle that was actually intended to limit retaliation—get even and leave it at that. We see it written in the Old Testament in Exodus and Leviticus.

> An eye for an eye, a tooth for a tooth, a hand for a hand, a foot for a foot, a burn for a burn, a wound for a wound, a bruise for a bruise. (Exodus 21:24 NLT)
>
> Anyone who takes another person's life must be put to death.
>
> Anyone who kills another person's animal must pay for it in full—a live animal for the animal that was killed.
>
> Anyone who injures another person must be dealt with according to the injury inflicted—a fracture for a fracture, an eye for an eye, a tooth for a tooth. Whatever anyone does to injure another person must be paid back in kind.
>
> Whoever kills an animal must pay for it in full, but whoever kills another person must be put to death.
>
> This same standard applies both to native-born Israelites and to the foreigners living among you. I am the Lord your God. (Leviticus 24:17–22 NLT)

Even before that, we see the concept mentioned in Genesis.

> And I will require the blood of anyone who takes another person's life. If a wild animal kills a person, it must die. And anyone who murders a fellow human must die. If anyone takes a human life, that person's life will also be taken by human hands. For God made human beings in his own image. (Genesis 9:5–6 NLT)

Now I would like to think that the world has changed since back then and we, as people, have evolved to a place of maturity beyond all of this, beyond revenge. Unfortunately though, I don't think we're anywhere close. In fact, before we jump into this, I want to make it clear that there will always be someone to forgive and there will always be an offense to overcome; you will never run out of opportunities to be offended in your life. That's just the reality of our human nature and fragility. What we do with that offense is up to us.

Back to the concept of an eye for an eye. While the literal eye for an eye is not something we see every day (or ever, I hope), the concept of revenge and retaliation is. Today's easiest and most accessible flavor of revenge is—drumroll please—social media! We feel slighted by someone—a person or an institution—and retaliate by speaking out against them, complaining about them, slandering them, or even threatening them to our online followers. We see celebrity feuds like this play out in front of our eyes all the time. Have I fallen for the clickbait? Absolutely. Have I gone into the comment sections to read all the chaos and all the back and forth? I'm not proud of it, but yes I most certainly have. People take to social media to rant and rage about whatever issue they're having with whoever managed to cross their paths that day. We complain about governments; we complain about bosses; we complain about bad drivers; we complain about ex-lovers and ex-best friends. It's all so public and so available for everyone to do and see. How do we not succumb to any of it? How do we shed the "eye for an eye" mindset? How do we give up our right to get even? How do we rise above it and truly love our enemies?

This is where we flip open our Bibles and head straight to the New Testament for answers. I don't think the answer will shock you, but the answer is Jesus. When Jesus came down from heaven and entered our world, He changed everything—including the concept of an eye for an eye.

Eye for an Eye

> "You have heard that it was said, 'Eye for eye, and tooth for tooth.' But I tell you, do not resist an evil person. If anyone slaps you on the right cheek, turn to them the other cheek also. And if anyone wants to sue you and take your shirt, hand over your coat as well. If anyone forces you to go one mile, go with them two miles. Give to the one who asks you, and do not turn away from the one who wants to borrow from you." (Matthew 5:38–42 NIV)

I mean He addresses it head-on, no beating around the bush. You used to do this. Now do this instead. Oh, how I wish it were that easy. We could talk about this portion of scripture forever, but I think the first thing we need to do after reading these new instructions from Jesus is something very difficult. It's not something we like to do. Once again, we need to lay down our pride. Are you sensing a theme here yet?

If you thought you were in for a bibbity bobbity boo kind of scenario (say a few magical words and all of sudden everything is fixed), I'm sorry to bring you back to reality. Loving our enemies, which includes forgiving them, more often than not, is hard work ... especially when it comes to laying down our pride. But how do we

Hard to Love

get there? How do we get to the point of forgiving our enemies in order to love them? First you need to ask yourself an important question: who is my enemy?

You may have a list of people in your mind already, names, offenses, and all the relevant details ready to go. But you may also not have a list. You may struggle to figure out who your enemy is because you don't feel like you have any enemies and that's OK. Granted, the word *enemy* can feel very strong so it might not be easy to think of anyone. That said, think about it this way: It could be someone who hurt you a long time ago and you're still trying to heal from the hurt and damage they caused. Or your enemy may not be someone who has harmed you personally. An enemy could be someone who hurt a family member or a friend. The truth is you may not even know your enemies personally. In fact, I'm going to challenge you and say that you have enemies that you don't even know you have.

It may be uncomfortable to put that label of "enemy" on someone you don't know (or even someone you do!), but you need to understand that enemies aren't just people you seek to harm and get revenge on. They can be people who don't necessarily threaten you but threaten your beliefs, your way of life, your social status, your public image, or your reputation. But the Bible tells us that we are to love those people. All people. *All people were created in the image of God.* (See Genesis 1:27.) It's easy to have that as head knowledge. After all, it's in the Bible. But if you're like me, it's not the first thought running through my head when I see an amber alert and the face of someone who has abducted a child on my television or smartphone screen. The fact that all people are made in the image of God is one of those things that can be incredibly challenging to move from head knowledge to heart knowledge. But stick with me; we'll get there.

The word enemy means the following:

- a person who is actively opposed to or hostile to someone or something;

- a thing that harms or weakens someone or something;
- someone who feels hatred for or engages in antagonistic behaviors against another;
- an adversary or foe.

Wow! Sounds like some really colorful characters! Lucky us, we get to love them! Notice I said "we *get* to love them" instead of "we *have* to love them." We don't *have* to love anybody. We don't *have* to do anything, in fact. That's the beauty of free will. God loves us so much that He gave us that gift. Although, if I'm honest, sometimes I wish He hadn't. It would make everything so much easier if we didn't have a choice. Can I get an amen? But free will *is* a gift. And *love is a privilege*. We *get* to love people. It's not always easy, but it is beautiful and we have a Creator who is willing to light our path as we choose to walk in love. Trust me: we need His help because we can't love our enemies on our own strength. I've been there, tried that; it doesn't work.

> But he said to me, "My grace is sufficient for you, for my power is made perfect in weakness." Therefore I will boast all the more gladly about my weaknesses, so that Christ's power may rest on me. (2 Corinthians 12:9 NIV)

We need Jesus. *Where we are weak, He is strong.* That's one of the most beautiful truths in the Bible. We don't think we can love our enemies because, let's be honest, the idea of it is absolutely ludicrous and completely contradictory to the status quo of the world around us. However, the truth is not that we can't do it; it's that we can't do it *alone*. We need Jesus and we need to trust that He knows what's best for us. He's never let me down, so why wouldn't I trust Him on this?

> Bless those who persecute you; bless and do not curse. Rejoice with those who rejoice; mourn

with those who mourn. Live in harmony with one another. Do not be proud, but be willing to associate with people of low position. Do not be conceited.

Do not repay anyone evil for evil. Be careful to do what is right in the eyes of everyone. If it is possible, as far as it depends on you, live at peace with everyone. Do not take revenge, my dear friends, but leave room for God's wrath, for it is written: "It is mine to avenge; I will repay," says the Lord. On the contrary:

If your enemy is hungry, feed him;
    if he is thirsty, give him something to drink.
In doing this, you will heap burning coals on his head.

Do not be overcome by evil, but overcome evil with good. (Romans 12:14–21 NIV)

Wow. That's a lot to take in. Now let's look to the wisdom book, Proverbs.

Don't say, "I will get even for this wrong." Wait for the Lord to handle the matter. (Proverbs 20:22 NLT)

Both in Romans and Proverbs, it's clear that God's got our back. We don't need to hold onto anger and unforgiveness because the God of the Bible is just and He is on our side. We don't need to get even; we don't need to waste our time stressing about it. We can focus on forgiveness and love because God's got the justice side of things covered.

Notice how in Romans 12:16, right after Paul tells us to bless those who persecute us and to live in harmony with others, he tells us not to be proud. Once again we are faced with the reality that before we can truly love others as we are called to, we need to lay down our pride. A big part of laying down our pride is recognizing that we can't do it alone. We need God. Another big part of it is grasping the realization that what people think about us doesn't change what God says about us. That's definitely worth repeating, but this time make it personal and say it out loud.

What people think about me doesn't change what God says about me.

You may not be familiar with this concept, but you need to get familiar and fast. Human nature tends to turn us into people-pleasers. When we become people-pleasers, we care more about what people think about us (popularity) than what God thinks about us and what He says about us. And I can personally testify that chasing popularity will always cost you your peace. It's not worth it. And it's a very slippery slope. Trust me. I've somersaulted down it many times. But when we turn our eyes to God, it doesn't matter what our enemies say or do. He can bring us through it. Jesus is our ultimate example of this.

Jesus doesn't just tell us to forgive our enemies. He demonstrates it for us through His own life and actions. To gain some context, let's start by looking at how He was treated.

> They shouted back, "Crucify him!"
>
> "Why?" Pilate demanded. "What crime has he committed?"
>
> But the mob roared even louder, "Crucify him!"
>
> So to pacify the crowd, Pilate released Barabbas to them. He ordered Jesus flogged with a lead-tipped

whip, then turned him over to the Roman soldiers to be crucified.

The Soldiers Mock Jesus

The soldiers took Jesus into the courtyard of the governor's headquarters (called the Praetorium) and called out the entire regiment. They dressed him in a purple robe, and they wove thorn branches into a crown and put it on his head. Then they saluted him and taunted, "Hail! King of the Jews!" And they struck him on the head with a reed stick, spit on him, and dropped to their knees in mock worship. When they were finally tired of mocking him, they took off the purple robe and put his own clothes on him again. Then they led him away to be crucified. (Mark 15:13–20 NLT)

Jesus, the only man to ever walk the earth without sinning, was beaten, spit on, mocked, and crucified. If anyone were to ever fall into the category of "enemy," the people who did this to Jesus would be top of the list. What Jesus went through was vile, cruel, and undeserved. It truly brings tears to my eyes knowing that He was treated this way. And after all the torture and humiliation, Jesus was nailed to a cross.

Two others, both criminals, were led out to be executed with him. When they came to a place called The Skull, they nailed him to the cross. And the criminals were also crucified—one on his right and one on his left.

> Jesus said, "**Father, forgive them**, for they don't know what they are doing." And the soldiers gambled for his clothes by throwing dice.
>
> The crowd watched and the leaders scoffed. "He saved others," they said, "let him save himself if he is really God's Messiah, the Chosen One." The soldiers mocked him, too, by offering him a drink of sour wine. They called out to him, "If you are the King of the Jews, save yourself!" A sign was fastened above him with these words: "This is the King of the Jews."
>
> One of the criminals hanging beside him scoffed, "So you're the Messiah, are you? Prove it by saving yourself—and us, too, while you're at it!" (Luke 23:32–39 NLT, emphasis mine)

"Father, forgive them." Even after everything, Jesus forgave and asked God to forgive His accusers, torturers, mockers, and murderers for what they were doing. He saw past their actions and saw them as children of God. Notice that even after He forgave, they continued to mock Him. It's unfortunate, but the truth is that forgiving someone doesn't really do anything for the other person. It doesn't change their behavior (as we see at Jesus's crucifixion). It definitely can, but it's not typically part of the package. We don't forgive for the sake of other people; we forgive because the people around us—our enemies included—are made in the image of God and God has commanded us to forgive. The healing that comes from that forgiveness is for you, the forgiver. Letting go of the hurt, anger, and offense cleanses your heart, not the other way around.

Reflection/Discussion Questions

- Does the thought of loving your enemies make you nervous or anxious?
- What do you think about the "eye for an eye" concept?
- Based on the definition provided, who could be considered your "enemy"?
- Have you ever struggled with a tendency to people-please?
- Journal or share your reaction to Luke 23:32–39 (NLT).

Chapter 15

REVENGE

So we've established that we have enemies. If I'm honest though, the word *enemy* still makes me uncomfortable sometimes. When I hear it, I see images of war, a battlefield, soldiers, the whole Hollywood movie deal. And while Hollywood images may be what I see in my head, the reality is that we are actually fighting a war. Every single day we wake up with air in our lungs, *we are fighting a war.* The devil is our biggest enemy, and he will use people to attack us and try to impose his will on us and our loved ones. We need to fight back. That's why Ephesians has the passage below:

> Put on the full armor of God, so that you can take your stand against the devil's schemes. For our struggle is not against flesh and blood, but against the rulers, against the authorities, against the powers of this dark world and against the spiritual forces of evil in the heavenly realms. Therefore put on the full armor of God, so that when the day of evil comes, you may be able to stand your ground, and after you have done everything, to stand. Stand firm then, with the belt of truth buckled around your waist, with the breastplate of righteousness in place, and with your feet fitted with the readiness that comes from the gospel of peace. In addition to all this, take up the shield of faith, with which you can extinguish all the flaming arrows of the evil

one. Take the helmet of salvation and the sword of the Spirit, which is the word of God. (Ephesians 6:11–17 NIV)

Why would we need armor if we aren't at war? We *are* at war; some of us just don't know it yet.

As I've already mentioned, I grew up with very low self-esteem. I never felt pretty enough, smart enough, or good enough. I was never enough. I constantly looked for approval from people. I craved any sort of attention, affection, and/or validation. Looking back at it now, my heart breaks for that broken girl who didn't know her worth. Who was so desperate to be loved but never felt like she was worthy of it.

As a young adult, I accepted Jesus as my Lord and Savior, and a few years after that, I faced a fight with an enemy that was unlike anything I'd faced before. The wildest thing about it all is that I still don't know who on this earth I was fighting (the actual person). I've never seen his or her face. I don't know his or her name. I have no idea why I was attacked, if there's even a reason behind it, or if I was the victim of a random act of cruelty. You might be a little confused and wondering what in the world I am talking about, so here is my story.

On and off for a couple of years, I had fake Facebook profiles pop up using my name and my pictures. I realize this will age me, but I was around when Facebook was first created and, at that point, none of us had any idea about privacy settings or any concept of protecting ourselves online or managing our online identities. It was just something new and something fun. I loved it because when someone liked my picture, I felt validated; I felt like I mattered. Isn't it interesting that twenty years later, people are still struggling with this? It's been a problem since the inception of social media! I have so much to say about that, but for the sake of my point, I'll get back to the profiles.

These fake profiles were using my name and my pictures and

they started claiming that I was doing amateur pornography. They were very aggressive in trying to "friend" people from my friend list, people I actually knew. To make matters worse, some of my so-called "friends" added these profiles, thinking it was me (yes, porn claims and all). It was beyond frustrating. I was mortified. I felt ashamed. People out there were believing these lies and there was nothing I could do! I kept reporting the profiles and asking others to report them as well. Eventually, years later, new fake profiles seemed to stop popping up. Finally, I could breathe again.

A few years after that, I happened to Google myself out of curiosity. When you have something like that happen to you, it's always in the back of your mind. It's hard to forget something like that—especially when it seemed so targeted—yet I never found out the rhyme or reason behind it all. Anyways, nothing—and I mean nothing—could have prepared me for the search results glaring back at me after I typed my name into the Google search bar and clicked "search." "What did you find?" you ask. Before I can delve into that, I have to ask another critical question. Have you ever heard of revenge porn? It's a much more commonly used term nowadays than it used to be. At the time of that Google search, I had no idea what it was. But believe me when I tell you I was forced to get well acquainted with it, and quickly.

I remember feeling my heart beat so fast that I could hear it. I remember my mind moving a million miles per second, unable to form a coherent thought or sentence. I remember feeling sheer panic, terror, and uncontrollable fear. I clicked on one of the links and this is what I found. A picture of my face with my name beside it. It was organized like a profile so it had my full name (first and last) and the city I lived in. It had blank spaces for more information, including where I worked, what gym I went to, my phone number, and other terrifyingly personal details. The main picture (beside the profile picture) was a photo of a girl with long, brown hair. She was naked on a bed and her phone was covering her face, taking a mirror picture. This was obviously very intentional because I knew the picture was not me but someone could argue it was because the face wasn't visible. I clicked on that photo and it took me to more naked pictures, claiming they were pictures of me, but none with the face visible. All the pictures had cameras or phones covering the person in the pictures' face so there was no reason for anyone to think they weren't me. They also had some real pictures of me scattered in with them (fully clothed, just selfies from old social media). It was, for lack of a better term, a porn profile.

Now as a side note, at this time in my life, I was a single woman and a friend of mine was planning to set me up on a blind date with a young adults' pastor. Well, to my surprise, this guy canceled our date before ever speaking a word to me, before ever meeting me, before anything. In fact, he convinced my friend to lie to me and break it off. (I guess that's better than a Post-it Note. Where are my SATC fans at?). Why? Because he Googled me. He assumed that I was naked all over the internet and doing porn. At the time, I was devastated. Not because of him—he was whatever and I thank God I didn't end up with him (Seriously, thank You, Jesus!). But I was devastated because someone in my circle had found this stuff. In my head, it was like a virus: once someone caught it (saw it), it would spread.

Needless to say, I was beyond horrified, broken, scared, and hurt. I just wanted to scream, cry, and hit everything in the room. This went on for a while. It progressed to the point that whoever was doing this actually went so far as to start photoshopping my face onto some of the pornographic images. I can't begin to explain how this new development destroyed me. Now there was nothing to keep people from believing these photos were of me. Everyone would think it was me because according to the internet, it was me. I'll also mention that when this all happened, photo editing was not as common as it is now. There weren't any apps to help. It took time and effort and not everyone could do it. Needless to say, I was fully convinced that my life was over. I had nothing left. Whoever was doing this had successfully destroyed me. They had won.

This was the absolute worst-case scenario for someone like me who had struggled with low self-esteem my entire life. The devil knew this, and he persisted. He had me trapped. Literally. I went through a period where I refused to leave my house. If I did, it was only out of necessity and I was convinced that every car on the road was following me. I assumed that whoever was doing all of this was laser-focused on finding out the details of my life (phone number, home address, etc.) to post on this profile so that all the sickos who saw it would harass me and make my life even more miserable. Because that's what this site did. In fact, they encouraged harassment and posted whatever personal details they could. At home, I would duck when I walked by a window in case someone was outside looking to confirm my address and post it. I was living in constant fear. It was a prison.

I eventually got so tired of it that I finally took it to God. What a concept, right? I definitely let it go on for longer than I should have, but when I tell you that the fear was all-consuming, I mean it. It was time to do something. After all, the book of Psalms says,

> The Lord is a shelter for the oppressed,
> > a refuge in times of trouble.
> Those who know your name trust in you,
> > for you, O Lord, do not abandon those who search for you. (Psalm 9:9–10 NLT)

How beautiful is that? He is our shelter and our refuge! I needed a shelter and refuge so desperately at that point so I ran to Him. I took some time to look up scriptures on fear and found one that spoke to me more than I can ever explain with words. After that, I spent days meditating on it.

> For God has not given us a spirit of fear, but of power and of love and of a sound mind.
> 2 Timothy 1:7 (NKJV)

In my desperation, my focus was rebuking the fear and claiming a sound mind. A sound mind was what I desperately needed. Confession time: I had never actually meditated on a scripture before this. I'd heard about it in sermons but I had never tried it. I didn't actually know how, if I'm being honest. But the word *meditate* means to actively engage in thought or contemplation; to reflect.

Think, contemplate, and reflect. I figured that was something I could do. So I sat on my floor. I read the scripture over and over and over again. I memorized it. I closed my eyes and repeated it over and over and over again. I visualized the words and emphasized different words as I repeated it. I became obsessed with this scripture, and I'm happy to report that it paid off.

As I continued to do these things, eventually the fear completely dissipated. God took away my fear and I finally felt like me again. I was free! Take that, fear!

God released me from that all-consuming fear and calmed the anxiety in my heart, which was beyond amazing. Through that entire experience, God taught me how to let go of the desire to gain the approval of people. But, and it's a big *but,* I will tell you with all honesty that I still hated whoever was responsible for doing this to me.

This whole situation happened long before I had kids, but in my house today, the word *hate* is a bad word. My kids don't use it because we've explained what a strong word it is and the implications that come with using it. We try to teach our kids love and kindness, and hate has no place in our lives. So when say that I hated that person, I don't take those words lightly and, while it may not be pretty and I may not be proud of it, it is honest.

This person—whoever was doing this to me—was more of an enemy than I could have ever imagined having. I saw them as pure evil. It felt as though they wanted me to suffer beyond imagination for every single moment of every single day. So once God got me through the fear, it was time to deal with my enemy. After all, I've got God on my side. My enemy has some wrath coming his or her way! Right?

Well, that's not exactly what God had in mind. I know the Bible says that God's plans are better than mine, but I was convinced in this particular instance I had a pretty good idea of what should happen to this person. That said, when I took it to God, do you know what He told me to do? He told me to pray for him or her. Ha! Not what I was hoping for. I was ready for God to bring out the lightning bolts and start smiting this cold, heartless, life-ruining person. But that's not what happened. He told me to pray for them. Ugh. This is the *worst*. I can't tell you how upset I was in that moment.

> But I say, love your enemies! Pray for those who persecute you! (Matthew 5:44 NLT)

The Greek word for persecute is *diōkō*, and it means to cause suffering, whether physically or emotionally. Whoever was responsible for putting me through this certainly caused me to suffer. So according to God's Word, I am to pray for those who cause me to suffer. Not the easiest thing to hear when you are in the midst of suffering ... In fact, it was the worst-case scenario in my mind.

However, bringing me out of the fear that I was in was nothing short of a miracle so I chose to trust God and vowed to do what He told me to do. The first time I prayed for this person is honestly one of the most vivid memories I have to this day. When I talk about it, I can feel every second of it all over again. It was one of the most excruciatingly painful experiences of my life. I was lying in my bed and started to pray. I started by asking God to bless whoever was doing this to me. I literally choked on the words as I tried to speak them. When I finally got the words out, I started bawling uncontrollably and my entire body contracted into the fetal position. My face contorted into my ugly cry face and I let out some silent screams. You know the ones where something hurts so much that you try to scream but no sound comes out because you have no breath or strength to push out the monstrous scream trapped deep in the pit of your soul? Yes, those ones. I felt intense physical pain and felt my heart shatter over and over again as I continued to ask God to bless this person and to change his or her heart. I prayed they would come to know God and experience His forgiveness and grace.

I did it. I did what God asked. I also did not mean a single word I prayed that night. Not one single word. I cried myself to sleep. When I got up the next morning, I did it all over again. I kept doing it, day after day (and it was a lot of days), until one day I was finally able to speak the words without crying. I still hated that person though. But I kept going. I kept being obedient and doing what God was asking me to do.

Eventually, something shifted inside of me and I could say the words without hate hiding behind them. Soon after that, I actually started to mean the words I was praying. I couldn't believe it! Through my obedience, God changed my heart. I mean He truly changed my heart. He took me from hating this person with every fiber of my being to caring about their soul and wanting the best for them. Only God can do that. He is still the God of miracles!

For me, *loving my enemy started with forgiving my enemy.* I let go of the hurt and the hate and I was able to move forward with my life. I gave up the power that hurt and hate had once held over me and I trusted an all-powerful God instead.

Life went on. A few months later, a friend sent me a link to an article containing an interview with someone who was essentially credited with creating and promoting the concept of revenge porn and the majority of the sites connected to it. In this interview, he said he had decided to shut down his sites and destroy all the pictures and information they had housed. That's a pretty big deal, especially because this person had always blatantly laughed at the criticism and hate and doubled down on what he was doing. When he was asked why he decided to shut things down, he said he'd had a change of heart.

Let that sink in. My enemy had a change of heart. The person who was at least partially responsible for undoubtedly the darkest time in my life, for the most horrific fear I had ever experienced, and who was responsible for doing the same thing to many other undeserving victims, had a change of heart. That is nothing short of a miracle if you ask me. That's God. Amazing what prayer can do, isn't it? Nothing is impossible for our God. David faced Goliath. I faced the internet. God was and will always be bigger than both. He is victorious. He is bigger than anything we can possibly face—yes, even the internet.

We also need to remember that God's Word is truth, nothing else. I had to dig into the Word and work on my self-love again after that incident.

Because that website said I was dirty, I was damaged, and I was ashamed.

God says I am washed clean, I am a new creation, and I am redeemed.

That website said I was worthless, my life was nothing, and no one would want me.

God says I'm worth dying for, I have a purpose and a calling, and I am loved.

The moral of the story is that with God's help, I learned how to love my enemy. Was it easy? Nope, not even a little bit! Do I want to go through it again? Not in a million years. Was it worth it? Absolutely, without a doubt.

Reflection/Discussion Questions

- How does the reality that we are fighting a war make you feel?
- When was the last time you put on the full armor of God?
- Have you ever run to God to be your refuge and shelter? Do you need to now?

- Have you ever meditated on scripture? Do you do it regularly? Journal or share your experience with meditating on scripture.
- Have you ever prayed for someone who hurt you or caused you to suffer? If so, how did you feel about it?
- Have you ever felt God nudging you to pray for someone? Have you ever witnessed prayer change someone's life? Prayer is such a powerful weapon in battle!

Chapter 16
HATE IS EASY

Hate is easy. Love is hard.

Love takes effort; it takes work.

Love is intentional; it needs to be on purpose.

The Bible tells us to pray for our enemies. But as I'm sure you managed to glean from my experience with revenge porn, that's not always something we *want* to do. And if I'm being completely honest, doing something you don't want to do is hard and inconvenient every single time. When someone hurts you so deeply that you just want revenge (we can even try to make it righteous by calling it justice), praying for them is probably the last thing on your mind. Think about it. We are more inclined to pray and ask God to get them a job on another continent, for something bad to happen to them, to make it all disappear, or even to do to them exactly what they did to us. As easy and tempting as those prayers may be, God won't do those things for us and it's because that's not His will and that's not what we, as Christ followers, are called to do. Trust me. I wish it were because that would be a lot easier.

If you're like me, the best advice I can give you in this situation is to fake it until you make it. I'm not usually an advocate for this strategy, but as I mentioned in the previous chapter, it worked for me in that particular circumstance—the circumstance where God was telling me to do something that I didn't want to do. It was the exact opposite of how I felt and that was hard for me. So when I started praying for the person who was actively trying to destroy my life, I was faking it. Actually, I should say that I was faking the sentiment behind the words I was praying. What I wasn't faking was my obedience to God. I did what He asked me to do even though I thought it might kill me. Seriously, I was in physical pain from the stress of uttering those words because everything in my body wanted the opposite of what I was praying for. Welcome to the battle of the flesh. But, and this is a big but, over time I stopped faking it and began feeling it. I don't know the exact moment when or how it happened, but it happened. I just continued to be obedient until one day my heart had changed. I am so glad we serve a God of miracles because changing my heart toward that person was just that—a miracle.

So after being harassed online with fake social media profiles spreading lies about me, my character—all of it—I had become a little paranoid. Can you blame me? And when I did that innocently curious Google search of myself, I wound up finding so much worse than the fake Facebook profiles, and I was understandably destroyed. What would people think of me now? I am not exaggerating when I tell you that I thought my life, as I knew it, was over. I thought that I would never get married (who would want me after that?) and I would never have a good job (what if a potential employer Googled me?). Yes, that seems dramatic, but what I didn't mention before is that whoever was doing this eventually took it a step further and started posting links to this stuff on the social media and blog posts of my former employer. They reached out to me and told me that this was happening and the posts were claiming that "the real Nikki" could be found at the links they were posting. As you can imagine, my former employer was forced to erase all mentions and connections to me or my name from all their website and socials. Not exactly a boost to the ol' self-esteem. I'll tell you that much.

All that to say that it became abundantly clear that whoever was behind these diabolical, perverse actions was actively and intentionally trying to ruin my life. There are no ifs, ands, or buts about it. And in that pain, that struggle, that catastrophic storm, Matthew 5:44 was nowhere near my train of thought. I was in full survival mode, fearing for my very life. You might think that's a little much, but remember this website had profiles of other girls with all of their personal info, including their home addresses, and comments encouraging people to harass them, stalk them, assault them, you name it. Whoever the nefarious owner of this site was, he or she, in my mind, was the absolute worst human being to ever walk this earth. I was in a Psalm 6 state of mind.

> I am worn out from sobbing.
> All night I flood my bed with weeping,
> drenching it with my tears.
> My vision is blurred by grief;
> my eyes are worn out because of all my enemies. (Psalm 6:6–7 NLT)

Beyond that, I was also really feeling the Psalm 7 vibe.

> Arise, O Lord, in anger!
> Stand up against the fury of my enemies!
> Wake up, my God, and bring justice!
> Gather the nations before you.
> Rule over them from on high.
> The Lord judges the nations.
> Declare me righteous, O Lord,
> for I am innocent, O Most High!
> End the evil of those who are wicked,
> and defend the righteous.
> For you look deep within the mind and heart,
> O righteous God.
>
> God is my shield,
> saving those whose hearts are true and right.
> God is an honest judge.
> He is angry with the wicked every day.

> If a person does not repent,
> God will sharpen his sword;
> he will bend and string his bow.
> He will prepare his deadly weapons
> and shoot his flaming arrows. (Psalm 7:6–13 NLT)

I have yet to see any flaming arrows—*that would have been pretty cool though, right?*—but God most certainly did not let me down. He is *always* faithful!

As I mentioned in the previous chapter, I went through a period of time where I was paralyzed with fear (and rightfully so). But when I decided that I'd had enough and couldn't live like that anymore, I turned to the Bible—God's Word—and meditating on 2 Timothy 1:7 broke me free from that soul-crushing cycle of fear and worry. That victory made me realize the importance of obedience.

Let's look at this for a moment. Just like love, obedience is hard. *Obedience is doing what we know we should do, even when we don't feel like doing it.* I can't address this without mentioning something that happened to me years ago because it really changed my perspective.

I heard a sermon by Joyce Meyer one day that completely rocked my world. It sounds so simple and obvious now, but at the time, it was life-changing for me. Through her teaching I discovered that my emotions are not from God. Our feelings are part of our humanity (flesh) and we need to overcome our feelings in order to make the right choices, the ones that align with God's Word (truth). Just look at Jesus! He didn't feel like being crucified. He wasn't excited about it. In fact, He asked God if there was a way out of it. But when it came time, He put his feelings aside, He did the will of God, and He saved my life and yours. For a long time Satan used my feelings to keep me out of God's perfect will for my life and he'll try the same thing with you. Maybe he's doing it right now. We all need to learn to overcome and look past our feelings and do what's right, what God's Word teaches, even if it's hard or feels uncomfortable at times.

I prayed for my enemy not because I wanted to, but out of

obedience to God. *Obedience must take precedence over our feelings.* As humans, we have feelings. That is inevitable. I'm not saying that's a bad thing. Jesus had feelings! He wept; He got angry; He got frustrated (with Peter, obviously); He felt human emotions. But Jesus's emotions were always passengers; they were never in the driver's seat. Jesus was always obedient to God and always aligned His actions with God's will. Again, Jesus is, and always will be, our ultimate example.

Someone else we can look at in terms of obedience is Noah. God told Noah to build a massive boat. Now we often imagine that Noah must have been mocked and made fun of or doing this, but there's no way for us to actually know if that was the case. It doesn't mention it in scripture so we are left to our imaginations as far as how Noah's neighbors reacted. However, Jesus did mention something about "Noah's days" in Matthew.

> When the Son of Man returns, it will be like it was in Noah's day. In those days before the flood, the people were enjoying banquets and parties and weddings right up to the time Noah entered his boat. People didn't realize what was going to happen until the flood came and swept them all away. That is the way it will be when the Son of Man comes. (Matthew 24:37–39 NLT)

It sounds like everyone around Noah was too busy or preoccupied with their own lives to chastise Noah for building a massive boat with no water in sight. I don't know which one would be harder: having everyone laugh at you or having everyone ignore you. That said, whether they thought he was foolish or not, building the ark would have taken an incredibly strong will partnered with some serious obedience. Think about it. Even if no one bothered to question him, seeing everyone else enjoying their lives, going to celebrations, having fun, and not slaving away building a massive boat (with no machinery to help!) would have taken some serious resolve. But that's who Noah was. Noah was obedient to God and he built the ark. He trusted God and was obedient when everyone else around him was living a different way. We need to trust God the way Noah did. If God tells us to love our neighbors and to pray for our enemies, that's what we need to do.

There is so much power and humility in obedience. Those two concepts (power and humility) may sound contradictory to you, but here's the thing: when we humble ourselves before the Lord, it makes room for God's power to abound. And who doesn't want more of God's power working in their lives?

Just like love, obedience is hard. Just like love, obedience is work. *Just like love, obedience is worth it.*

But how do we become obedient?

I think the best place to start when it comes to being obedient in loving your enemy is to search your heart for hatred. Sounds fun, right? Well, it's not. It's actually a little terrifying. But it is helpful.

> Search me [thoroughly], O God, and know my heart;
> Test me and know my anxious thoughts;
> And see if there is any wicked or hurtful way in me,
> And lead me in the everlasting way. (Psalm 139:23–24 AMP)

David was a man after God's own heart. He had a deep desire to be right in the sight of the Lord, and we see that in the scripture above.

God already knows our hearts. He knows everything! But a lot of the time, we need to be open and willing for Him to actually be able to reveal those things to us; otherwise, what He has for us will fall on deaf ears. So this is where we start. We have to be open to discovering any lasting feelings of hurt, any grudges, any preconceived notions, prejudices, feelings of hate, all the ugly shadows that may lie in the depths of our hearts. You may have years of offenses built up or a few little shadows that you haven't dealt with yet. Either way, we all need to be checking our hearts constantly. Like I said, life is full of opportunities to get hurt and offended. Checking our hearts needs to be something we do throughout our entire lives, even when everything is "good".

When I do this exercise myself, God usually ends up showing me things that I thought I had already dealt with or moved past, things I didn't know were still there. But I've learned to always listen and when I lean into what He shows me, He is always right. Well, duh. I need to address those things again, be more thorough, and get to the root of the hurt. More often than not, what I have discovered is that the anger or hurt that I was holding against another person was usually rooted in something bigger: lack of self-worth, fear of rejection, unmet expectations, etc. I mean really heavy things. And yes, there have also been instances when someone has deeply wounded me with their actions and, while I've moved past the things they did and don't wish them any harm, I also wasn't wishing them any good. Praying for them was hard, which I will tell you now is a sure sign that you still need to do some work.

So I challenge you to take a page out of David's life, straight out of the book of Psalms, and pray,

> Lord,
>
> I humbly come before You now with a genuine desire to be obedient to You and to be more like You. I ask that You please search my heart and reveal to me anything that is not of You. Please show me anyone that I need to forgive and if there is any unforgiveness or hate in my heart.
>
> In Jesus's name, amen.

Pray this in the morning and throughout your day (if you remember). You may have thoughts that pop up throughout the day or you might bump into someone who reminds you of someone who hurt you. Just trust that God will answer your prayer and be ready for what He shows you. Eventually, this prayer/practice should become a habit. This prayer should be a regular prayer in your life as you walk with God.

One example of this in my own life is I had an ex-boyfriend who I broke things off with and he did not take it well. He was really mean about it. I will spare you the details, but the relationship was not healthy and I blamed him for a regression in the progress I'd made in specific areas of my life. He didn't respect my boundaries and I was hurt deeply by the realization of what he did to me and it was not something I took lightly. I wanted everyone to know what he did and how he was fooling everyone around him, living a big fat lie. But I knew that wasn't what God wanted me to do so instead I prayed and asked God to help me forgive him. I found myself repeating the words "I am choosing to forgive _____" on a daily (sometimes hourly) basis. Honestly, I felt like I was failing at forgiving. At least, that's what I thought every time I had to repeat the forementioned sentence. But I kept at it, out of obedience: *pray, forgive, repeat.* After some time, I became apathetic toward him, meaning that I didn't think about him and I let go of my desire for revenge (in this case, to shout from the mountaintops what he'd done). After all, Paul tells us in the book of Romans,

> Dear friends, never take revenge. Leave that to the righteous anger of God. For the Scriptures say,
> "I will take revenge;
>   I will pay them back,"
>   says the Lord. (Romans 12:19 NLT)

So I kept being obedient, praying, and forgiving, and after some time, I was able to pray blessings over him. Even now as I write this,

I intentionally left out a lot of the details because, while I haven't named this individual, there are people in my life who will read this and know who I am referencing. As such, I've chosen to keep the details private because, with God's help, I've moved on from that and don't want anyone to hate him or hold a grudge against him because of me. I'm now actively protecting the person who deeply wounded me. That seems ludicrous, right? It's definitely countercultural but that's our God! Trust me: nothing is impossible for God.

Love your enemies.

Reflection/Discussion Questions

- Have you ever had to "fake it 'til you make it"?
- What does it mean to be obedient to God? Do you struggle with this?
- Do your emotions tend to be in the passenger seat or the driver's seat?
- When you prayed the prayer in this chapter, did God bring anyone to mind that you need to forgive?
- Have you ever "failed at forgiving"? What did you do? Did you keep trying, or did you give up?

Chapter 17

FORGIVENESS, THE REAL MVP

If you've made it this far through the book, you may have already discovered that I can be a bit dramatic (unintentionally, of course). However, while this next sentence may sound dramatic, it's not; it is completely honest and true. If you can learn to forgive and love the people who have hurt you, who have wronged you, who have offended you (your enemies), your life will change. Girl Scout's honor. (Even though I was never a Girl Scout, I believe this is as good as a blood oath, right?) Seriously, if you can do this, your life will change.

What I mean by that is your perspective will shift. Your heart will change and it will heal. You will create space for God to do amazing things in your life. You will see people differently. You will see God differently. You will see yourself differently. Your relationship with God will grow. Like I said, your life will change, and it will change for the better.

I'm sure you've heard the saying "Unforgiveness is like drinking poison and expecting the other person to die," and it is so incredibly true. Holding on to unforgiveness gives the person (or people) who hurt you power in your life. How? Because they control your emotions, they keep hate and anger in your heart. They occupy your heart and your mind. And hate never stays put. It always spills over into other relationships and other aspects of our lives, often without us even realizing it.

If I take a moment to think about all the people who have hurt me, offended me, or betrayed me throughout my life, the last thing I want is to give them power in my life. In fact, the notion of willingly giving them any power, thought, or feeling is outrageous! If you agree with me, this is where we need to take a stand, realize it's unhealthy to live in unforgiveness and anger, and do something about it. But don't just take my word for it. Let's look at what the Bible says.

> And "don't sin by letting anger control you." Don't let the sun go down while you are still angry. (Ephesians 4:25–26 NLT)

When we are consumed with anger for someone, it controls us. God says to resolve it before the sun goes down. Essentially, if you're mad, deal with it before you go to bed so you can wake up tomorrow, a new day, and move forward.

> Get rid of all bitterness, rage, anger, harsh words, and slander, as well as all types of evil behavior. (Ephesians 4:31 NLT)

It's not good for us to have bitterness, anger, and rage in our hearts. I think anyone and everyone would agree to that! In this scripture, it also says to get rid of harsh words, slander, and evil behavior as well. Isn't it interesting how those things are all connected? If you have bitterness, anger, or rage in your heart, it's inevitable that it will spill out into your words and your actions. Once it does that, it starts permeating every aspect of your life to some extent, including your relationships and how you love others.

> Whoever says he is in the light and hates his brother is still in darkness. (1 John 2:9 ESV)

Hard to Love

We can say that we are Christian, we love God, and we follow Jesus, but if we aren't doing what's commanded of us by God, we're just fooling ourselves. Our words are just words. It's time to step out of the darkness and into the light!

> Human anger does not produce the righteousness God desires. (James 1:20 NLT)

God doesn't want anger in our hearts. It's not righteous. It's not what He, our loving Father, wants for us. God wants the best for us, despite our sinful nature. He wants us to be spiritually healthy and happy!

> If anyone says, "I love God," and hates his brother, he is a liar; for he who does not love his brother whom he has seen cannot love God whom he has not seen. (1 John 4:20 ESV)

This is a bold statement and a real wakeup call. If you hate someone, you can't love God. Think about that for a minute. This is a life-changing scripture right here. *We can't love God if we hate people,* and we can't get rid of the hate in our hearts until we forgive.

> But I say, if you are even angry with someone, you are subject to judgment! If you call someone an idiot, you are in danger of being brought before the court. And if you curse someone, you are in danger of the fires of hell. (Matthew 5:22 NLT)

I think this one speaks for itself. Pretty straight-forward stuff.

> But if you refuse to forgive others, your Father will not forgive your sins. (Matthew 6:15 NLT)

Again, it's eye-opening to see the importance of our obedience on this subject. *Our forgiveness from the Father depends on us forgiving others.* Wow. This is one that, for me personally, I've had to hold on to and really meditate on when I've struggled to forgive. In some ways, it terrifies me, and in another way, it comforts me. I know that sounds contradictory, but let me explain. My deepest fear is one day standing before God and knowing that I disappointed Him or that I could have been so much more, done so much more for the kingdom. And this scripture plays into that fear for me. The other side of it is that this scripture reminds me of how much God has forgiven me (and continues to forgive me) for, and it's comforting to know that no matter who I need to forgive or what I need to forgive them for, it can't possibly be as much as God has forgiven me. It gives me hope. "I can do this. With God by my side, I can do this."

> Hiding hatred makes you a liar;
> slandering others makes you a fool. (Proverbs 10:18 NLT)

It's important that when we have hatred, anger, or bitterness in our hearts, we deal with it. Notice how I said *when*, not *if*. We will all be hurt and offended in our lifetimes because not one of us is perfect. Growth and progress come from recognizing what we're feeling and dealing with it instead of burying it or running from it. We can't pretend it's not there; we can't hide it. If we do, we are lying to ourselves, just like it says in Proverbs.

Luke 8:17 (NLT) says, "For all that is secret will eventually be brought into the open, and everything that is concealed will be brought to light and made known to all."

We can't hide from God.

As you can see, the Bible has a lot to say about hatred, anger, and unforgiveness. There are more scriptures on these topics than the ones listed here, but for now, I'll leave you with these and hopefully you discover the rest on your own. The point of me including these scriptures is so that you can see, beyond the shadow of a doubt, that God does not want us to have hatred, anger, and unforgiveness in our hearts, no matter how badly someone has hurt or wronged us. It's poison, just like the old saying goes. God even goes so far as to say that if we refuse to forgive others, He won't forgive us. That's a really big deal.

It is critical for us to recognize that hatred, resentment, and everything related never stay isolated. It taints our hearts and that spills over into our lives in ways we may not have expected. If you have unforgiveness in your heart for one person, chances are you might develop some resentment toward a mutual friend who still spends time with that person. Or you meet someone with similar characteristics and immediately judge them based on your past hurt. That doesn't seem fair when I put it like that, does it? It's also important to remember that if you have kids, they watch and learn from us. We simply can't let them learn hate from us.

Now I want to mention something that is very important when it comes to forgiving people who have hurt us because I don't want you to misunderstand what forgiveness is.

Forgiving is not forgetting. Contrary to the popular "Forgive and forget" saying, forgiveness doesn't necessarily have to go hand in hand with forgetting. When I say that you need to forgive, I'm not advocating putting yourself in harm's way or allowing yourself to be hurt over and over and over. That is not forgiveness. Forgiveness is letting go of the hold someone else has on you. It's letting go of what they did. It's realizing that they are a broken person in a broken world. *Forgiveness is giving up your right to get even.* It is giving up your right to hold the offense against them. Forgiving doesn't mean you need to trust them again. It doesn't mean you need to give them any of your time. It doesn't mean you have to be their best friend or even talk to them ever again. Forgiveness just releases the anger, hurt, and resentment in your heart toward that person. It frees you. That is why forgiveness is such an important part of our walk as believers because, as we've seen in the scriptures, forgiveness is being obedient to God.

As for how that will change your life, if you want specifics, I can tell you that it gives you a new level of freedom. Who doesn't want that? Letting go of anger, hatred, and unforgiveness will increase your peace and deepen your relationship with God. Sign me up!

Another thing that the practice of forgiveness will do is give you back your time. Have you ever wasted time being angry at someone? I'm raising both hands, both feet, and if I had more limbs, I'd raise them too. Like I mentioned earlier, I used to always have imaginary arguments in my head or replay an encounter with someone and all the things I should have said or done ... what a waste of time. God didn't put us on earth to waste our time like that. So once we build forgiveness into our lifestyle, once we make it a habit (yes, forgiveness can become a healthy habit), it changes our lives in so many different ways.

All this talk of forgiveness may be making you nervous because of how deeply someone hurt you, and hey, you may not feel ready to forgive. Well, I can tell you that there's no right or wrong time to forgive. You just need to do it, whether you feel "ready" or not. You don't have to *feel* like forgiving someone to actually do it. (I am exhibit A for this concept.) Forgiveness isn't about our feelings; it's about being obedient to God and releasing something in your life that is weighing you down. Again, don't just take my word for it. Jesus makes it so clear. We can't ignore the need to forgive.

> Parable of the Unforgiving Debtor
>
> Then Peter came to him and asked, "Lord, how often should I forgive someone who sins against me? Seven times?"
>
> "No, not seven times," Jesus replied, "but seventy times seven!
>
> "Therefore, the Kingdom of Heaven can be compared to a king who decided to bring his accounts up to date with servants who had borrowed money

from him. In the process, one of his debtors was brought in who owed him millions of dollars. He couldn't pay, so his master ordered that he be sold—along with his wife, his children, and everything he owned—to pay the debt.

"But the man fell down before his master and begged him, 'Please, be patient with me, and I will pay it all.' Then his master was filled with pity for him, and he released him and forgave his debt.

"But when the man left the king, he went to a fellow servant who owed him a few thousand dollars. He grabbed him by the throat and demanded instant payment.

"His fellow servant fell down before him and begged for a little more time. 'Be patient with me, and I will pay it,' he pleaded. But his creditor wouldn't wait. He had the man arrested and put in prison until the debt could be paid in full.

"When some of the other servants saw this, they were very upset. They went to the king and told him everything that had happened. Then the king called in the man he had forgiven and said, 'You evil servant! I forgave you that tremendous debt because you pleaded with me. Shouldn't you have mercy on your fellow servant, just as I had mercy on you?' Then the angry king sent the man to prison to be tortured until he had paid his entire debt.

"That's what my heavenly Father will do to you if you refuse to forgive your brothers and sisters from your heart." (Matthew 18:21–35 NLT)

OK, that last verse though ...

Just in case you needed more proof that we need to forgive. If we can't forgive others, we can't fully accept God's forgiveness. And not being able to accept God's forgiveness, mercy, and grace is very problematic to our walk as Christians, as I'm sure you would agree. If we look at the breadth of sins that God has forgiven in us and in others, they could never compare to anything someone else did to us. Never. It's impossible. I understand that because of our human nature and our emotions it may feel like the end of the world when someone hurts us, but the truth is it's not. It's OK to feel our emotions, but we still need to focus on God throughout it all and fully submit every situation to Him, just like Abraham did. One thing I know from experience is that God is faithful and if we press on and we move forward, He will be right there with us every step of the way.

> I consider that our present sufferings are not worth comparing with the glory that will be revealed in us. (Romans 8:18 NIV)

> "For I know the plans I have for you," declares the Lord, "plans to prosper you and not to harm you, plans to give you hope and a future." (Jeremiah 29:11 NIV)

> I press on to reach the end of the race and receive the heavenly prize for which God, through Christ Jesus, is calling us. (Philippians 3:14 NLT)

He is faithful and wants what is best for us. We can take comfort in that.

> Make every effort to live in peace with everyone and to be holy; without holiness no one will see the Lord. (Hebrews 12:14 NIV)

Do to others as you would like them to do to you.
(Luke 6:31 NLT)

Homework time!

Challenge

Pray and ask God to bring to mind someone who you dislike, someone who has hurt you, someone who might be considered your "enemy" or someone that you are still holding bitterness, resentment, or anger for. Then pray for that person. That's it. Ask God to bless them (this can be a lot harder than it sounds) and work in their life. Repeat this every day for a week and see if you feel any differently toward that person. If not, keep praying that same prayer for another week and ask God to soften your heart toward them as you do. Ask Him to help you see that person as He sees them. Ask for God goggles.

Reflection/Discussion Questions

- Out of all the scriptures listed in this chapter, which ones stands out to you the most?
- Do you feel like any of the listed scriptures challenged you or convicted your heart?
- Do you find Matthew 6:15 terrifying or comforting?
- Journal about or discuss the parable of the unforgiving debtor.
- Did you complete the challenge at the end of the chapter? How did it make you feel?

Chapter 18
FINAL THOUGHTS

We've all been through a lot; it's part of life. Love is also part of this life. But love, real love, has God at the center of it. After all, God is love. So as we learn to love ourselves, love God, and love others—including our enemies—we must keep grounded in our faith, ask God for strength and guidance, lay down our pride, and approach it all with humility. It takes work and won't be easy. But if you've gotten this far into this book, I trust that your heart is in the right place and you have a genuine desire to love. For that, I applaud you. Put in the work, dig deep, and trust the One who created it all. It will be hard at times, but you can do it!

I want to leave you with some words from a five-minute mini sermon I was asked to give at my home church a little while ago. It wasn't what I had planned on speaking about, but God led me in a different direction than I had planned. He does that a lot and I couldn't be more grateful! I ended up speaking about love and compassion for others because of the incredible way my daughter exhibits these traits in her life. I hope this touches your heart as it did mine when God led me to share it with my church.

A couple of weeks ago, we were at Michaels grabbing some picture frames and my kids (four and five) were all over the place. They were running, they were wrestling, they were rubbing their hands along anything and everything … It was a challenging outing,

Hard to Love

to say the least. We'd asked them to stop fooling around probably three or four times because we didn't want anyone to get hurt, but their selective hearing must have kicked in and the shenanigans continued. Well, my daughter (the oldest) decided to piggyback her brother. Let me preface this by saying that my son is a very solid little dude. So in the back aisle of Michaels, about 10 feet from where we were standing, we heard a loud crack followed by an even louder scream. My husband and I turned around and my daughter had tried to get my little guy on her back but couldn't hold him so she went straight back and the loud crack we heard was my little guy's head, his sister landing on top of him. Because his hands were wrapped around his sister's neck piggyback style, he couldn't put his hands back to brace himself as he fell. It wasn't good. We rushed to him. Meanwhile, my daughter stood there crying and screaming, just as loud as her brother. Now she wasn't hurt at all, and in the moment, I was frustrated—not just because they didn't listen to us and someone got hurt, but because I needed to give my full attention to the child who had smashed his head on the ground and was actually hurt. We were checking for signs of concussion and bleeding and trying to comforting him at the same time. I didn't have the capacity/patience to deal with, what seemed in the moment as, attention-seeking screaming too. Anyone else ever get frustrated with their kids? I hope I'm not the only one.

We got out to the car and my little guy had stopped crying. He was sitting in his car seat reading a Batman book, but my daughter was still sobbing. This sweet, little girl that I am so blessed to call mine told me that she was just so sad that her brother was hurt and that she wished she could do something to help. My frustration instantly melted away. And honestly, it's so true to her character. This tiny, little human has always had giant-sized empathy in her heart. Even from two or three years old, every time we would watch a movie or a show and she saw someone who was sad, got hurt, or wasn't treated kindly, she has always cried. Not a single tear—full on bawling. And it's not because she's trying to make it about her. It's not that she wants attention. It's because her heart genuinely breaks at the hurt of others, at the pain she sees others going through. It's such a beautiful quality, and I never want to discourage that in her.

In that moment, God used her to teach me a lesson, to show me that my heart toward others has become a little hardened, even somewhat cynical. The COVID-19 pandemic certainly didn't help. For two years we were told to avoid human interaction at all costs. It's hard to connect with people when you can't be around them. Do you have a heart for people or has it been hardened like mine had? Maybe past experiences have taught you that it's just easier to do nothing than to deal with the messiness of people. Honestly, it's easier to ignore, to avoid, to dismiss people and their hurt. Don't get caught up in the mess. But is that what we should be doing? Should we beeline for the exit after a church service instead of stopping to meet someone new? Would Jesus do that?

How often do we pray, "Lord, break my heart for what breaks Yours"? If we pray that and we hold on to that conviction, if we tap into the empathy that my baby girl shows every day, we, the church, the body of Christ, could truly change the world. If we saw everyone we encounter through God's eyes, with empathy, mercy, and grace, how different would this world be?

John 13:35 (NLT) says, "Your love for one another will prove to the world that you are my disciples." It doesn't say by our preaching, by how many scriptures we have memorized, by how many times a day we pray, how many days a week we're in church. *"Your love for one another* will prove to the world that you are my disciples."

One of the values here at my home church is "Love is our answer." Love was Jesus's answer on the cross. Love is the answer to a broken relationship with God; salvation is love. So join me today, and let's ask God to give us a passion for people. And as we pray, "Lord, break my heart for what breaks Yours," I pray that God would continue to soften my heart and all of our hearts for His children, for people. Let's love each other as my little girl loves others.

If I could speak all the languages of earth and of angels, but didn't love others, I would only be a noisy gong or a clanging cymbal. If I had the gift of prophecy, and if I understood all of God's secret plans and possessed all knowledge, and if I had such faith that I could move mountains, but didn't love others, I would be nothing. If I gave everything I have to the poor and even sacrificed my body, I could boast about it; but if I didn't love others, I would have gained nothing. (1 Corinthians 13:1–3 NLT)

Reflection/Discussion Questions

- Which part of the book stood out to you the most (Love Yourself, Love God, Love Others, or Love Your Enemies)?
- What is your biggest takeaway from this book?
- Is there anything from the book that you want to dig deeper into or look into further?